For Caroline

Allegro assai e un poco agitato

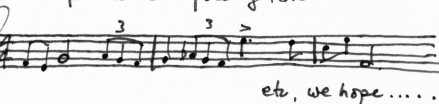

etc, we hope.....

with love   Tom   x

Sept. 5ᵀ 1986

Disasters in Concert

Disasters in Concert

Compiled by
TOM EASTWOOD

With a Foreword by
THE EARL OF HAREWOOD

Illustrations by ffolkes

A Nadder Book

ELEMENT BOOKS LTD

Printed in Great Britain by
Billings, Hylton Road, Worcester

Designed by Humphrey Stone
Jacket illustration by ffolkes

Contents

Foreword

All performance is a comment on what is performed and an act of communication with the audience. If things go right, the audience should be borne aloft towards the heights and, with luck, the performers will follow them. If things go wrong, there is no limit to the depths of horror, sometimes extremely comic, to which we may all plunge.

In the Opera House I have more than once watched the curtain go up at the right moment and then immediately start to descend. Usually the performance re-starts – once, memorably, in a "Rhinegold" at the Coliseum when the warmed-up horns were much better than usual the second time – and once, lamentably, also at the Coliseum, when the curtain never achieved its required ascent before Act III of Iain Hamilton's admirable opera "Anna Karinina" and that audience went away with only two thirds of the music heard and the action shown. That was a disaster.

So was the first time I ever heard Bartok's sonata for two pianos and percussion, many years ago in a small hall in London. When we got there, the person responsible for arranging it said that fate had struck – twice. First of all, the two percussion players had not looked at the music before rehearsal. As there was no question of them learning it in time, he started to rearrange the programme. But fate struck again as the pianists would have none of it and decided to play their parts and tap the piano and perhaps the piano stool, clap their hands, bang their foreheads and do almost anything to imitate the sounds the percussionists should have been making. The results beggared description.

Perhaps that particular work, magnificent as it can be, is accident prone. It was I think in the first year I was responsible for the Edinburgh Festival that John Ogden and his wife, Brenda Lucas, were about half-way through the sonata (with well-rehearsed percussionists) when I noticed that pins were falling out of her carefully braided hair. She tried to stem the flow but the result was that quite a lot of the sonata was for only one and a half pianos and percussion, which wasn't quite what we had hoped for. So well however had the first part gone that I could think of only one remedy, which was to ask them to play it again the following year. They did, admirably, so perhaps the gremlin was exorcised.

Those occasions I witnessed, but my preferred episode amongst those I didn't witness was told to me autobiographically by my brother-in-law, Barry Tuckwell. He was playing Benjamin Britten's Serenade for Tenor, Horn and Strings on an LSO tour involving a number of different cities. Well on in the tour, and having been faced a number of times already with the problem posed by the epilogue (off-stage, dying away, finishing *ppp*), he found the perfect solution. At the back of the hall, there was a lift big enough to take a grand piano and into it he went for those last soft phrases. At the concert he did the same, only for the lift to descend almost as soon as he got into it. His colleagues found the result magical, but were surprised when he reappeared on the platform after a long delay in a state of some exhaustion, quite unexpected in someone so experienced!

Disasters will recur, embarrassments continue to harass the profession, but it will be a sad day when musicians cease to regale their friends and colleagues with new and horrendous tales of catastrophe, each one documented and of course ascribed to the teller's closest rival.

HAREWOOD

Preface

First, grateful thanks to all those artists who have given their time and trouble to contribute their favourite worst experiences to this book. There could not have been a book without them, so never was such an acknowledgement more literally true. Special thanks to Miss Söderström and BBC Radio 4 for permission to reproduce her contribution. To those who could not contribute, or to those I did not dare approach, I can only say, if you see a copy, please feel encouraged to let us have a story for a possible Volume Two.

There have been other 'disaster' books, of extreme success, but what I think makes this one a little different is that nearly all the stories have come direct from the people themselves. That makes them incontrovertibly true, it goes without saying, but it also means a fascinating picture of a personal reaction to a situation, and a sudden lighting up of what can be going on behind that perfect performance we all take for granted. A myriad of mischiefs have threatened the performances in this book, from earthquakes via gaol to ducks.

If audiences seem to come off badly, let me redress the balance. They are a sporting lot. They may giggle if things go wrong, but in the end there is nothing like a good disaster, brilliantly surmounted, to bring out the best in them. A mauvais 'moment musical' means extra warm applause at the end. In our rapidly changing world one can at least hang on to that.

I am particularly glad that this book will, in its turn, be making a contribution to the Royal Society of Musicians. This wonderful organisation helps our profession when we get into difficulties, and it is good to be able to reciprocate in some way.

On the other hand, there are some kinds of difficulty which could defeat even the Royal Society. Please read on.

TOM EASTWOOD

The Consort of Contributors

Flute	Gareth Morris
Oboes	John Anderson, John Cruft
Clarinet	Gervase de Peyer
Bassoon	William Waterhouse
Horn	Barry Tuckwell
Xylophone	James Blades
Celesta	Betty Matthews
(non-playing)	
Piano Septet	Vladimir Ashkenazy, Susan Bradshaw, Louis Kentner, Moura Lympany, John McCabe, John Ogdon, Roger Vignoles
Harp	Sidonie Goossens
Harpsichord	Lionel Salter
Tanpura	Basil Douglas
Guitar	Rose Andresier
Sopranos	Jane Manning, Rosalind Plowright, Elisabeth Söderström, Dame Eva Turner
Mezzo Sopranos	Nancy Evans, Sarah Walker
Tenors	Sir Peter Pears, Robert Tear
Baritone	John Shirley-Quirk
Lute Singer	Martin Best
Violins	Hugh Bean, Iona Brown, Peter Carter, Ida Haendel, Emanuel Hurwitz, Yehudi Menuhin
Violas	Katharine Hart, Christopher Martin
Cello	Julian Lloyd Webber
Double Basses	Barry Guy, Rodney Slatford
Organ	Gillian Weir
Conducted by	Daniel Barenboim, Sir Charles Mackerras,

	Roger Norrington, Sir John Pritchard and Karlheinz Stockhausen
Guest Narrators	The Earl of Harewood, Michael Vyner for the London Sinfonietta, Beresford King-Smith for the City of Birmingham Symphony Orchestra
Répétiteur	Richard Nunn.

Audiences

Audiences are important for the ingenious ways they can find to distract the performer. We are not thinking so much of people who cough, scrape their chairs or suddenly want to go home. These are fairly routine concert-poopers. The artist tends to ignore them (unless he is **Paul Tortelier,** who politely called out "Au revoir, Madame!" to a lady who left when he was in the middle of a phrase).

Talkers can be more dangerous. They usually converse in low tones while the music is soft (rather like people in church), but can be badly caught out if, say, there is a fortissimo build-up followed by a pause. Then their confidences spill over into the silence with ruinous benality. One thinks of that famous moment in the Albert Hall, when out of a breathless hush came a woman's voice saying "Personally I always wrap mine in newspaper."

Categories of audience more dangerous yet have menaced our contributors and their predecessors, some striking at the roots of the self-confidence that should emanate from the platform:

(a) *Audience ridiculously thin on the ground*

If an audience cannot even get itself into double figures, there is obviously something wrong somewhere. The performer may conclude, quite wrongly, that there is something wrong with himself. An ensemble can always console itself with some *sotto voce* gallows humour. Not so the solo artist, even the great **Benno Moiseiwitsch.** One cannot imagine his feelings when he was fulfilling an engagement to play on a pier, and after a long walk in freezing rain in the general direction of France, sat down to give a recital to an audience of three.

He might have cheered himself up, I suppose, by thinking that, in certain circumstances, three is a crowd. But one doubts it.

(b) *One or more of the audience apparently certifiable*

This has been the experience of two of our contributors. We open with **Michael Roll** and his Nordic saga. The prelude is a story of its own:

It was in February 1983 that my luck ran out, in Helsinki's Finlandia Hall. The concerto was supposed to be Mozart's K 482 (the work I had prepared) but I soon spotted a poster declaring it to be Beethoven's 2nd, while a yearly programme book was suggesting Mozart K 503! We settled for Beethoven's 3rd concerto, which I had played elsewhere the previous week.

It was half-way through the first movement that I noticed them. 'Them' (or they) were a young couple sitting about eight rows from the front, and obviously something hilarious was taking place and affecting them accordingly. I immediately jumped to the cause of their mirth – I was pulling faces, the sort that many pianists pull, only worse. This had most definitely precipitated their sad plight, and from then on my concentration became severely tested.

At the end of the first movement I opted for a long icy stare in the direction of the offending couple. Suitably chastised, they made worthy efforts to disappear under their seats without ever quite achieving it, and by the time the third movement was under way they had 're-infected' each other, and from then on there was no looking back for them, or sideways for me.

The concert was repeated the following night. In the knowledge that lightning cannot strike twice, I allowed myself a preliminary peep at the audience out of the corner of my eye. To my absolute amazement and indeed horror there 'they' were again. They were sitting in exactly the same seats (perhaps they had stayed there overnight). I couldn't believe it – I was dumbfounded.

Somehow I managed to concentrate on the concerto for most of the time. The occasional lightning glance revealed them to be behaving with considerable restraint. Only in the coda did the male member of this terrible duo give in to his true feelings, and he buried his face in his handkerchief for the final page or two of the concerto.

They displayed surprising enthusiasm following the performance, and that did nothing to help me resolve what will always be a burning question: did they ever return for another performance of Beethoven's No. 3, or was it the side-show that was too good to be missed?

Audience categories (a) *and* (b) seem combined in what one might call the 'Branden Syndrome' as experienced by **Robert Tear**. Once again the introduction, though founded on different material, is inseparable from the Gothic scherzo that follows:

Imagine this. An orchestral tour to the Far East, and an exhausting one. We aren't flying straight home, certainly not. We are flying to Winnipeg, we will take a bus into Manitoba – Branden, Manitoba to be exact. There is a centenary there or something. We will give our second programme; that's the one in which I sing *Les Illuminations* de Britten.

That glorious hysteria that glues itself around the dog-tired was simmering. Already on the plane we had spent two Sundays (the date-line plays sporty jests with time) and had been surrounded by what seemed like the whole of the oriental neophyte stock wailing as one. The surrealistic experience of an immense journey from the Orient, followed by a two-hundred-mile bus trip, increased the simmering to a bubbling.

At last Branden. We're changing. The conductor (a certain Raimondo Gattopardo who shall remain nameless) puts his foot through the arse of his pants, and begs for ink to blacken his underclothes. Bubbling . . . almost boiling.

My turn. Out I go and see a hall full of empty seats. There are perhaps five or six people right at the back, one of whom is the orchestral manager. There is one person about half-way down on the left, and in the front row, exactly in my eye line, an old crone with black teeth and a loony expectant look.

We begin and continue. I get (half-way through the piece)

to my exquisite pianissimo glissando at *Et je danse*. There is a sudden shriek of hysterical laughter as if the inhabitants of bedlam were on a day trip to an echo chamber. In front of me, hooting in obvious near ecstasy, head thrown back, rocking in her seat, is the sole soul of row A.

The conductor, with suppressed laughter, weeps torrents of tears through the rest of the piece. The girls with the fiddles and cellos hide behind their long hair. The manager can be seen in the aisle with a handkerchief in his mouth. The stage heaves with mirth . . . I can't sing – only bellow and hope.

Boiled!

(c) *Audience, in part or in whole, unable to appreciate music at all*

This has nothing to do with business sponsorship of the arts. It is the extraordinary situation the late **Jo Spanjer** encountered, and her husband, Paul Amphlett has very kindly given us the story:

The setting was a mission hall in East London, where Miss Spanjer was to give a concert for the elderly. The chairwoman led her on to the stage, and announced as follows:

"I must apologise to Miss Spanjer, who has so kindly agreed to play for us, for the condition of the piano, which has seen better days." (This was the understatement of the century. It was already apparent that there was a metal spike sticking up where middle C should have been.) "And I would especially like to tell her," went on the chairwoman "that the front two rows of the audience are both blind and deaf, but they know she is here, and are very pleased to have her with us."

On this inspirational note, Miss Spanjer sat down to give her recital. The piano was far sicker than anyone could have imagined. The middle C spike was the mere tip of the iceberg. If one avoided that, one landed on another note which made no sound, or if it made a sound, it was beyond redemption out of tune.

The audience was unworried, though. The front two rows talked loudly at each other throughout the performance.

(d) *Ansa-Bak audience (indigenous to Australia)*

Before encountering this audience at Woollongong, New South Wales, **Martin Best** and his Consort had a nasty experience in the dressing-room. The venue was an old theatre, presided over by a nice young man* in a white tuxedo:

> He greeted us tenderly and showed us the dressing-room, into which we clattered with our endless supply of instruments. Suddenly one of the group – I can't remember who – went quiet and pointed to the ceiling. There, plain as a pikestaff and minding its own business upside down, was a

> large tarantula. We all clustered round, making unprintable comments through clenched teeth, and were becoming wrapped in fascinated amazement, when it suddenly moved.
>
> Until one has experienced the effect of six already slightly unhinged musicians trying to get through a door at once, the phrase 'rush to the exit' is a mere figure of speech. The nice

---

*As we shall see, nice young men seem to feature in tours.

young man came to investigate the welter of arms, legs, bows and flutes flying round the backstage area. He tried to calm us down by saying that the insect in question was "only the baby," but that "the mummy must be somewhere near". And we still hadn't begun the concert.

The programme started with some exquisite 13th-century songs. For these to be fully effective, a quiet trance-like atmosphere has to be created in the hall. From the first moment it was clear this was going to be impossible.

The auditorium was equipped with iron-framed tip-up seats. The noise they made when sat down in was considerable. As most of the audience was late, it was through the sound of these seats descending that we had to perform. It began to bring to all of our minds a previous occasion, which I won't go into, but it had involved performing in the garden furniture section of a department store in France.

This memory, combining with what was happening now, and with the recent tarantula experience, began to cause a serious breakdown in the composure of my bass player, standing just behind my left shoulder. His stifled heaves of laughter did not help Bernart de Ventadorn's journey from medieval Aquitaine to 20th-century Woollongong. Also, in the distance, at the back of the hall, I could see the Chief Usher, a tall, thin man with a thin grey moustache. He wore an ancient dinner-jacket with medal ribbons on its breast pocket, and deemed it necessary to check up at frequent intervals on the state of affairs in the foyer. Each time he opened the door to look, a shaft of light fell on his face and illuminated the back half of the audience, most of which was in motion, accompanied, of course, by the noise of the seats. In about the fourth row, the head of EMI Australia's classical division was already giving a fair imitation of my bass player.

As I launched heroically into the lovely 'Ai, tan grans enveya' with which Ventadorn expresses his desperate passion, I felt a sort of hopelessness come over me. I ground to a halt at the end of the phrase, pausing to draw breath and trying not to laugh. As I did so, I caught the eye of an aggressive-looking fellow in the second row. He had his arms folded and a gleam in his eye, and with deep interest I saw his mouth open.

"Look, mate," he called out loud and clear, "you ain't gonna get more Antipodean than *this*."

For the English equivalent, here is a story of my own. I was at an open air performance of *Faust* in Finsbury Park. The soprano playing the part of Marguerite was a big girl, and when she obeyed a stage direction to faint, it was quite a noticeable moment. The man next to me was impressed. "Blimey!" he exclaimed, "She fell like a Venus on a rock-cake!"

Débuts and Early Days

The artist newly arrived, or newly arriving, has some of the charm of the new-born foal, a little unsteady on his legs, engagingly awkward. One thinks of **Michael Roll** slipping up and sending the conductor crashing into the orchestra pit, as he tried to shake his hand. One thinks of **John Cruft** sitting down on a chair which instantly collapsed as he made his first orchestral appearance as an oboist. One thinks of **Gillian Weir's** début – but that was so intimately linked with a page turner, that we ask you to turn the page to that section (p.ooo).

You don't always have to make the conductor fall into the orchestra pit to enliven your début. There are other objects you can send there as well. **John Shirley-Quirk** showed that at his first appearance at Glyndebourne:

> As a début, it had a certain involuntary aspect. Mr Shirley-Quirk was still a full-time teacher of chemistry at Cambridge, and was engaged by Glyndebourne to understudy the part of Mittenhofer in Hans-Werner Henze's *Elegy for Young Lovers*. There was the usual last-minute theatrical cliff-hanging; Glyndebourne needed the vocal score until two weeks before the production.
>
> Despite this, Mr Shirley-Quirk got himself to the stage of being able to read the part ("just about" in his words) but obviously in no way able to sing it all by heart, let alone give an actual performance in the role.
>
> Came the night, and the singer playing Mittenhofer lost his voice. Crisis, but a compromise was reached. The voice-less singer would act the part, Mr Shirley-Quirk would sing it from the music.
>
> He was therefore ensconsed, front of stage, with a heavy, ornate Victorian music stand, and sang while **Carlos Alexander** acted away. As often happens, the audience quite quickly became used to a novel convention, and all

went very well. Mr Shirley-Quirk just had to move the music stand a little, to see the conductor, but had no particular difficulty in his voice-over role, which he fulfilled with great success.

As he walked off, however, he found too late that the small adjustment he had made was a dangerous one. The first act curtain swept up the music stand and flung it into the pit, where it landed with a fortissimo crash on top of the timpani, causing, we understand, some damage.

Mr Roll's conductor had landed among the first violins. One does not know which orchestra suffered the most dilapidation from a début.

The great breakthrough (no allusion to the last story) can have its moment of anticlimax – one can breathe easy too early, as **Julian Lloyd Webber** discovered:

I woke with a sense of excitement. By the end of the day I would have made two important débuts – my first performance in Holland and my first ever television appearance.

It had all begun more than a year before, towards the end of my student days at the Royal College of Music. Dutch Television had contacted all the British music colleges and auditioned hundreds of aspiring young soloists, myself included, for their new series *Brilliant Young Musicians from around the World*. It would be a marvellous opportunity as the programmes had built up massive audiences. When a letter arrived with the news that I, along with two singers, had been chosen to represent Britain, I immediately started agonising over what I should play for such a vital occasion – it would have to be something pretty impressive.

The television people decided for me. They particularly wanted Haydn's Concerto in D, one of the hardest pieces in a cellist's repertoire – with a finale which had become a legendary graveyard for nervous performers.

Having understandably failed in my repeated attempts to get Haydn changed to Shostakovich I set about my practice fiendishly, and by the time I left for Amsterdam, Haydn had been the cause of temporary insanity among most of the

occupants of my block of flats, and had driven the rest out altogether.

Thoroughly prepared, I longed for the moment when it would all be over, and I could relax again.

After several days more rehearsal in Holland, preparations were complete and, as I took the platform, I felt a strange sense of calm – *tonight* nothing was going to go wrong. My confidence grew and grew, and by the time the finale arrived I was thoroughly enjoying myself – negotiating its notorious pitfalls with ease. A storm of applause greeted the last chords and, after taking my bows, I was embraced by a beaming producer, who pronounced the performance 'perfect'.

Elated I packed up my cello and set off for the bar and a celebratory drink. Now there's nothing quite like a long glass of beer to make up for sweat lost during a concert, and by this time I felt I'd earned more than usual. Several long glasses later the producer, still beaming, arrived beside me, seemingly to join in my celebrations.

"The performance was magnificent," he declared, "We've watched the whole thing through and you were just wonderful." My senses reeled both with pleasure and increasingly severe inebriation. He continued. "But we had a little trouble with the pictures towards the end, and I'm afraid there's no alternative but to take the finale again. Please be back on the studio floor in five minutes."

A nightmare fear that besets all artists came true for **Susan Bradshaw,** just when she wanted to make a good impression:

My worst experience was one shared with Richard Rodney Bennett. In 1958 we were asked by Cologne Radio to record three pieces for two pianos he'd completed the previous year while we were both students in Paris, and which we were due to play at the Darmstadt Summer School the following week.

We set off in some excitement to fulfil our first professional duo engagements, taking the cheapest possible route on the overnight boat *The Holland*. One of our fellow travellers was an American, also bound for Cologne, who offered us a lift in exchange for the promise of conversation to keep him awake on the journey, and thus we arrived at our destination in the late afternoon, sleepless, but with plenty of time to find a hotel and have a short rest before the recording at eight o'clock in the evening. Deciding to meet in an hour's time, we retired to our separate rooms.

The next thing I knew, I seemed to be in the middle of a nightmare. It was certainly the middle of the night – one o'clock in the morning to be precise – and there I was, lying on my bed, dressed and ready to leave for the radio station *five hours* too late! Paralysed with horror, I looked round to see Richard standing in the doorway. He, too, had just woken up!

Our explanations for absence, made in halting German, were, perhaps understandably, somewhat coldly received. We thought we would never live it down, but they did in the end invite us to return ten days later!

Does this sorry tale merit inclusion? It doesn't seem all that terrible now, but at the time we thought we'd die of shame. And I've been particularly careful *never* to go to sleep before concerts ever since!

For a tense, breathless race against time, calculated to a split minute, involving road, rail, and air, international timetables and a trio of principals in different countries, the story of **Rosalind Plowright** and her Hamburg State Opera début is a suspense thriller hard to beat.

On Friday evening, 13th March 1981, Leonie Rysanek cancelled a performance of *Ariadne auf Naxos* scheduled for the Sunday. The Intendant of Hamburg State Opera, trying to replace Miss Rysanek in a hurry, knew that Rosalind Plowright was singing Ariadne on Friday night at Frankfurt. He left an urgent message for her there, but it never got through. Finally, in desperation, on the Sunday morning of the performance, he telephoned Tony Kaye, Miss Plowright's manager.

"Why didn't you ring me first?" asked the manager. (They always ask that, but rightly in this case.) "There may be something I can do."

There was. Her itinerary showed she would at that moment be on a train between Frankfurt and Brussels. He checked with Cook's International Timetable. Her train would make a stop at Cologne at 10.07. It was now 10.03. He picked up the telephone. Miss Plowright takes up the story:

I remember I had my head in the score of Beethoven's *Missa Solemnis* when we pulled into Cologne Station, and I could not believe my ears when the station Tannoy started to blurt out *"Frau Plowright bitte, Frau Plowright bitte..."* This can't be for me, I thought. No one knows I'm here. I went back to my score, but a few seconds later the Tannoy started again. "Frau Plowright *bitte*, get off ze train, Frau Plowright..."

I realised it must be for me after all, and was very annoyed. A few moments before I had been sitting there comfortably engrossed in my score, and now here I was lugging my heavy suitcase off the train, convinced that something dreadful must have happened. Things hardly improved when I found my way to the station-master's office, and was told that I should ring my manager in London and that it was very urgent. I had no German money with me, but the station-master very kindly let me use his phone, and I rang Tony in London.

Tony explained. "Leonie Rysanek is ill, and has cancelled tonight's performance of *Ariadne* in Hamburg. Can you do it?"

I was in a terrible fluster, and all sense of calm had left me. My train had just pulled out of the station. It would be about three hours before the next one arrived, and I had no German money on me. I just burst into tears. Tony asked me for my number at the station, told me to hang up and calm myself down, and then rang me back a few minutes later.

By that time I had pulled myself together. There was no reason why I could not sing Ariadne. After all, I had sung it only two nights before. I had had a day off, and would have plenty of time to warm up before the performance, especially since Ariadne does not really sing until the second half of the opera.

When Tony rang back I told him I would do it, but that I

had no way of getting from Cologne to Hamburg because of having no money. "Don't worry about that," Tony said. "That's Hamburg's problem. Just stay by the telephone."

A few minutes later, the phone rang again. This time it was the Intendant of the Hamburg Opera saying how grateful he was. He told me to take a taxi from Cologne to Düsseldorf Airport, where I could catch a Lufthansa plane which was due to leave in just over an hour.

It was not all good news, however. The performance was apparently due to start at 6 pm and not at 7 pm. This really shook me, as it was clear I wouldn't be able to do as much warming up as I'd hoped, but there was no getting out of it now.

I still had no money, but I did have one Eurocheque left. The Intendant told me to go to the local hotel, where he would arrange for it to be cashed. This I did, and once armed with money and the good wishes of the hotel staff, I found a taxi which took me to Düsseldorf Airport just in time to catch the plane. Met at Hamburg Airport, I was taken straight to the Opera House for a costume fitting. Then the stage director showed me around the set, and from there I went upstairs to warm up my voice.

I checked into a hotel, and half an hour later I was back in the theatre to be made up. Unbelievably, at 6 pm I was on stage in a production of *Ariadne* that was completely new to me.

At the beginning of the second half, I forgot my first line (ironically *"Wo war ich?"* "Where was I?"!) but the rest of the performance went very well, and the Hamburg audience were very kind to me. When I think about it now, I realise that I never really quite knew what was going on, but the experience did me no harm. It was, at the very least, a rather unusual way to make one's début at a major international opera house!

Two generations of musicians know **James Blades** as the master of any percussion instrument you can think of. Yet fifty-four years before Miss Plowright's Hamburg début, he was having teething troubles with a xylophone, which won him another appreciative audience. One might even say it launched him:

During my sixty-one years of professional 'percussing' I have, like most musicians, encountered terrible moments, most of which I try unsuccessfully to forget.

One of my most embarrassing experiences occurred as far back as 1927 (!) in the Caird Hall, Dundee. I was at that time employed in the orchestra of the Kinnaird Picture House, an eight-piece ensemble, which provided the musical background to the then silent films.

For a special presentation of an epic silent, *The Better 'Ole*, the manager of the Kinnaird rented the Caird Hall, and I moved over to provide the sound effects required, *and* to play a xylophone solo in the intermission. My expertise on the xylophone was, to say the least, somewhat suspect, but I *could* manage a modest galop, and 'Annie Laurie' played first as a ballad, and then in the current 'raggy' rhythm (no doubt quite 'raggy').

The Caird Hall was packed at every performance, particularly on the opening night, when 'Royalty' was present.

After the customary newsreel and short comedy film came the intermission; my xylophone was wheeled to the centre of the stage, and I made my way to the wings awaiting my cue to make my début.

At the given signal I attempted a dignified entry, but had the ill luck to trip up over the wire leading to the panatrope, which resulted in my charging headlong to the centre of the stage. To bring myself to a halt, I thought to steady myself on my xylophone, which, rather than assist me, decided to add to my mortification by rolling down-stage and finishing upside down in the footlights.

Something prompted me to bow discreetly to the boxes on my left and right, in which the élite were seated. They kindly acknowledged my bow with a gentle applause, which was taken up at full strength by the entire audience, giving time for two hefty stage hands to retrieve my instrument. After solemnly shaking hands with the two helpful Scots, I attacked my xylophone with vigour and speed, and was given an encore.

At the end of the evening I was about to apologise to the manager, but he got in first, saying "Splendid! What a marvellous way you made your début!"

Dress

Even if it breaks the law, we have to make a sexual discrimination here.

Men

Basically, the situation with the men is that they have lost or forgotten some essential part of the white tie and tails equipment *de rigueur* for the platform, while the women find themselves in entirely the wrong dress for the occasion. This is no reflection on either sex, it just happens. There are interesting variations to the rule, such as **Daniel Barenboim** meeting a Greek concert producer clad only in bathing trunks and an Arab head-dress, and, for the added complication of conductors putting their feet through the seat of the pants, please look under **Robert Tear** on page 3. On the subject of trousers, there is a rather nice story which the agent, **Basil Douglas** relates about **Trevor Pinnock.**

It was at the Santiago de Compostela Festival (incidentally a bit of an agent's *pesadilla*), and Trevor Pinnock was directing the English Concert at a church, manned, if that is the right word, by nuns. For some reason Mr Pinnock had tied his trousers up with string, which was hanging out through the tails of his coat. Basil Douglas, like a good agent, duly tucked in the string. The nuns took this to be a fatherly gesture, and after the concert congratulated him on the performance of his son.

Roger Vignoles at one moment, actually found himself without trousers at all. Do you cancel the concert, or take a chance and go on as you are? Luckily, there was a Good Samaritan on hand, who drove fifteen miles home to lend him a pair. Roger Vignoles has in fact been extremely resourceful in making a whole gamut of essentials re-materialise, right down (or up) to cuff-links, which he regards as no problem – "If the worst come to the worst one can use safety-pins or even paper-clips."

One item fazed him though – a white tie. He found that hard to track down, even in a public school.

It was a problem also for **Barry Tuckwell,** and he was nowhere near a public school:

> I recall arriving in Milan for a recital minus certain essential pieces of concert dress – tie and waistcoat. I was not unduly concerned as I thought I would be able to borrow these at the hotel. Unfortunately the restaurant was closed for renovations, and the waiters were on holiday.
>
> OK, I thought, I am playing at La Scala, and they must have five thousand ties and waistcoats. No, this was not a possibility as the wardrobe was closed. This was an important concert and I wanted to look reasonably tidy, so I improvised. I made a tie from a British Airways napkin from the plane, carefully hiding the name. For a waistcoat, I just took a towel from the hotel and made it into a cummerbund. Actually I looked pretty good. I still to this day carry my British Airways reserve tie – just in case.

Solved – *campana in aria*! But Mr Tuckwell rightly makes the point that one must not assume these things are always available. Some hotel towels, for instance, have colours totally unsuitable for the concert platform – green, orange.

Louis Kentner came up against a sartorial problem on tour in the United States. He calls it 'A Winter's Tale', and the occasion is a piano recital in one of the American universities:

> It had been a harsh winter, and snow and ice were still lying everywhere. I was advised to buy myself a pair of galoshes. The only ones I could get were quite disgusting – dirty white plastic things, but I had no choice in the matter.
>
> When I started my recital I noticed that the audience were tittering, which puzzled me as I was not aware that there was anything funny about my performance of Schubert's 'Wanderer' Fantasy. But when I glanced downwards I saw the reason: I had forgotten to take my galoshes off.
>
> Suppressing my own desire to laugh (or cry) I finished the performance, the galoshes taking an active part in the pedalling, then I left the platform, making squelching noises as I did so.

When I returned – without the galoshes – the audience gave me an ovation.

Women

Vive la différence! Even so a lot of the trouble has come from dresses, beautiful in themselves, which turn out not to be the right ones to play in. It soon dawned on **Gillian Weir,** beginning a programme with the Bach Organ Prelude and Fugue in D, that her new silk dress had the effect of her being seated on a glissando. Pedalling up the big scale, – bottom to top of the console – that starts the work, she found the part of herself which was swathed in silk sliding uncontrollably along the organ bench. With the last note, she slid off the end. (Note: Bach never intended this. He would have made some indication.)

On another early occasion – after a tremendous, triumphant thrust at the end of 'Transport aux Joies', she broke a strap, and had to leave the stage of St George's Hall, Liverpool, precipitately.

"These days," she says, "I try the dresses out first." By the results, she certainly does, and I wish I had seen the all-sequin dress she wore to open the new organ in San Francisco.

Added troubles worried the guitarist **Rose Andresier.** We find her wearing a blouse with voluminous sleeves, a long skirt, and with a dreadful cold. She has tissues galore stuffed up the sleeves. Making her bow, she feels the popper go on her skirt:

> I had never yet lost a skirt in front of seven hundred people, and even though I was wearing a long white petticoat, I didn't relish the thought of losing it now. I sat down, started to play, sniffed (I hope discreetly) and when it was time for me to stand again, I took my bow, forcing my elbow against my waist. All was safe. However, I eventually needed to blow my nose. I felt up my sleeve. Right sleeve, left sleeve, nothing! I was desperate. All I recall of the remainder of the concert was my sniffing every time I played a forte, and bowing with my elbow forced against my waist.
>
> The concert was reviewed – and well at that – to my utter amazement. The review was entitled "Rose's Fresh Fruits". I had never felt less 'fruity' in my life.

Miss Andresier's paper handkerchiefs had got wedged in her waist! Heaven knows what she was playing.

Dame Eva Turner was emphatically wearing the wrong dress for the occasion. But it was very much *force majeur:*

> It happened a long time ago, but when I look back on the occasion I can always laugh!
>
> It was in 1928, and I was endeavouring to return from England from Las Palmas, where I had been to open the newly built Perez Galdos Opera House with performances of *Aida* and *Il Trovatore*. Immediately following on this engagement I was scheduled to be at the Royal Opera House, Covent Garden, by a certain date in order to start the rehearsals for *Turandot* where I was to make my début in that opera in the International Season of 1928.
>
> Means of travel were in no way as easy as they are today.

The delay in the opening of the Perez Galdos Opera House had alas! put my schedule out, and I was really 'on the spot' to find some way whereby I could get back to England.

Imagine my consternation to find there was no ship scheduled which could get me back in time, and it was only by dint of the kindness of the managing director of the Elder Dempster Line at Las Palmas that I was able to make it.

There was a cruise ship stopping for a few hours to enable the passengers to visit the local Yacht Club for a dinner dance – one of the attractions of the cruise. The captain happened to be a friendly colleague of the Elder Dempster official. That very evening I had to sing my last performance of *Il Trovatore*, and the captain of the cruiser said he would take me on board provided I could make it by a certain time.

It really was quite a scramble; no time to take off my make-up, or change out of my last act costume. I just had time to climb up the rope ladder from the tender, with my long-haired wig and my *Trovatore* robes flapping in the breeze. The passengers on board were all hanging over the side of the ship, (*The Arcadia*, by the way) wondering what on earth was coming on board. The laughter was hilarious.

However, notwithstanding I had to pay for the round trip of the cruise, I breathed a great sigh of relief and I 'made it'. Thus started my long association with the opera *Turandot* at the Royal Opera House, Covent Garden.

Embarrassments and Misunderstandings

Never the twain shall meet

It is difficult to get the great together, as **Lord Harewood** illustrates in this story.

I am reminded of the genuine horror which overtook Ben Britten when he gave a concert in (I think) 1949 in Los Angeles, conducting an orchestra which he didn't know, and which wasn't very good. He was abject with nerves and was, he told us, sick in the interval, which was one of his normal reactions to such situations.

A few weeks later, Erwin Stein got a letter from Schoenberg saying he had tried to see Ben at the interval of his concert, but he had apparently been drunk and was unable to receive anyone! But then Schoenberg always did believe the worst of everyone.

Déjà vu

Another example of mind not quite meeting mind, is the encounter between **William Waterhouse** and Messiaen – the second encounter at that.

One of my more embarrassing moments occurred during a visit by the distinguished French composer Olivier Messiaen to the BBC studios to supervise the rehearsing of one of his works by the BBC Symphony Orchestra, of which I was then a member.

Thinking that this would be a good opportunity to get his autograph, I brought along to the rehearsal a copy I happened to own of his *Chronochromie*, and during a break took it to him, asking him if he would inscribe it for me. He said that he would be pleased to do so, and, taking my score, looked for a suitable page.

"Mais, il est déjà signé...!" There, staring at him, was the

signed dedication he had written for me on the occasion of a previous visit, about which I had obviously failed to remember very much...

Get Well Card

Gillian Weir, (incidentally once introduced on an American television programme as 'one of the world's greatest organisms', which embarrassed the interviewer but not her) found herself in verbal trouble in a church in Albany, New York.

People have a way of being carried out of her concerts (her report, not ours), overcome, presumably, by her organism. On this occasion, one of the audience had a severe heart attack. The para-medics went into action at the back of the church, and over the bleeping of their monitoring system, Miss Weir decided to chat to the audience and keep things calm until the patient was removed.

A good way to do this was to start giving some verbal programme notes on the next piece in the programme, which was by the French 'organism' Vierne. She told them what an interesting life he had had, and an even more interesting (now, too late, she saw where she was going) *end* to his life. Because it was his last recital at Notre Dame, he had been given a theme to improvise on (no going back now) and after giving it out he fell, well, dead at the console. Seeing this was hardly the right note to be striking, she strove for an up-beat ending. With earnest gaiety she said, "Wasn't that a *wonderful* way to go!"

The patient was carried out.

Other contributors have been embarrassed on a much more pedestrian level (literally), finding difficulty in either getting on or getting off the stage.

In general, it seems true to say that concert platforms have not always been designed with easy approaches. (The architect was perhaps over-influenced by the classic advice to aspiring artists, that the way to the concert platform is 'Practice, practice, and more practice'.) It is especially true for ladies in recital dresses.

The five or six steps to the platform at the Royal Festival Hall are notorious. You will notice that when a lady soloist is negotiating them, the applause stops, to be renewed again when she has safely arrived. The same applies to men when they reach a certain seniority, such as Stravinsky in his later appearances there. The involuntary silence watching the ascent, the relief of the audience that the artist has reached the summit without disaster, show that the concert-goer has his heart in the right place; but there is still something wrong with the design.

Things are well-nigh impossible if you try and approach the platform from the *auditorium*. You are not meant to of course, but sometimes you have to.

Hugh Bean, playing the Bach E major violin concerto at Twickenham, nonchalantly tossed his bow into the audience on the first note. Nobody made any effort to return it to him (they seemed paralysed), so he had to hop down and retrieve it himself. Once down, he found he could not get back, unless he was a kangaroo. The shelf of the rostrum towered like a cliff. He tried

putting a leg over, but the height ruled out any question of an elegant two-point landing. The only thing to do was to throw his bow on to the platform, put one knee up, then lie on his stomach,

perilously close to the edge, before regaining the upright position by a kind of extended press-up. As he did this it became
apparent that it had been a long time since anyone had cleaned
the floor. He played the concerto covered in dust.

Any difficulty in getting *off* the stage is extremely embarrassing,
because it upsets the whole system of applause. Unless people
know you cannot find the exit, they will be puzzled that you keep
reappearing, and do not seem willing either to give an encore or
to tear yourself away. The clapping becomes lifeless, and a nasty
vision arises of the audience silently filing out, while the artist
goes on withdrawing and returning on the stage. Even if the
reason is clear to everybody, it does not help. It is no comfort to
be forced to play the lead in some kind of farcical *bonne-bouche*.

Thoughts such as these might have been occurring to **Iona
Brown**, as she tried to leave the stage of the Teatro Real, Madrid.
When the moment came to make the decisive exit, she found the
door leading off the stage would not open. She accordingly came
back to make an extra bow, but when she went off again, it still
would not open. Back she came once more, only to find on her
third exit, that she was still sealed in. She came back a fourth
time...

Finally the door was unlocked. It was just as well the janitor
knew no English.

John Anderson, at the Purcell Room, had to suffer full audience
participation:

I was giving an extremely serious and highbrow recital of
contemporary and avant-garde music in the Park Lane
Group's series. The first piece was one I had written myself,
and was unaccompanied. The following work was with
piano accompaniment, and so I asked the backstage hand to
open the door for me to leave the stage after I had finished
my short opening number.

I went on, and rather nervously played my short piece,
which received a little polite applause. I turned round to
leave the stage. To my horror I saw that an enormous curtain
was in place all across the back of the stage, so that not only
was there no open door, but no door to be seen at all. In

addition I couldn't see where the join in the curtain was, to attempt to find the door.

So, with my toes curling with embarrassment, I began to grope my way along the curtain to try and find a way off. The audience had been pretty calm until then, but of course giggles, then laughter and cries of amazement ensued. Someone shouted "Left a bit!" Then the door opened, some distance from where I was, and everybody clapped as I rushed out.

Of course the doorman hadn't heard the applause after my piece, and thought it was still going on. However, he did wonder why everyone was laughing.

Elisabeth Söderström's experience is of another dimension altogether. In earlier times her song might have ceased upon the midnight, rather abruptly.

A ladies' club in Sweden once asked me to come and give a concert on a very special occasion. Our Queen Luise, sister of Lord Mountbatten, was going to attend an evening meeting, and the ladies wanted me to sing a special programme of her favourite songs.

The room where I was going to sing was not very large, and as every member of the club wanted to attend this evening, the chairs filled every inch of the floor. The Queen was going to sit in an armchair about a yard away from where I had to stand next to the piano. I rehearsed, worried about being so close to the audience, but tried to cheer myself up with the fact that my voice was in very good shape that evening.

I was waiting in another room listening to the expectant chattering of the ladies taking their seats. Then, silence when the Queen arrived, a welcoming speech, and one of the ladies came to tell me that it was time for my concert. I walked into the room, stopped in front of the Queen, and made the traditional deep curtsy demanded by protocol.

I did not know that, after my rehearsal, the ladies had put a small table on three legs just behind the place where I stood. When Queen Luise arrived, she had been presented with a large bouquet of flowers. On the table there was a vase full of water, into which her flowers had been put, to keep them fresh during the evening.

When I curtsied, my rear end hit the table, and the vase and its contents dived straight into the lap of our dear Queen. The ladies stood up as one man with a scream. I stared at the mess I had caused. The Queen was a lady with a wonderful sense of humour. She started a giggling laughter, which developed into the nearest to a roar of laughter a queen would allow herself. She stood up, and I tried to help. We both left the room, and it took quite a while to get her dress dry enough for her to sit comfortably through my programme. I would have understood perfectly if she had been angry and left, but instead she treated me most kindly, and the concert was one of those unforgettable ones – before and after each song we looked at each other and giggled.

It is lucky for musicians that the laws about *lèse-majesté* are now a little more relaxed. **Gareth Morris** recalls the final rehearsal for the Coronation Service in Westminster Abbey in 1953, when an emissary of the Earl Marshall appeared, to give each member of the orchestra the royal invitation (and pass) for the ceremony the next day.

We were placed in the large organ loft above the rood-screen. The magnificent embossed cards were handed to each of us as we sat there; but as the flautist Geoffrey Gilbert (who was next to me), took his, it fluttered from his hand, and disappeared between the floorboards into the bowels of the organ, never to be seen again.

It must be quite rare for a royal invitation to be swallowed by a musical instrument, especially an organ.

Half-time

John Ogdon was playing a programme in the Konserthus, Gothenburg. He had just come to the end of the pretty exacting Fifth Sonata of Scriabin, when a ruddy-faced Swede strode masterfully on to the platform and called out "CANADA 3, SWEDEN 1." This was puzzling. If there was any question of scoring, it should have been GREAT BRITAIN 3, RUSSIA 3. Not that one shoulder enter upon a recital in that spirit. One does not play a composer with the idea of knocking him out in the third movement. We all wondered what he meant, but it transpired that an important ice-hockey game was in progress...

In that case, it is a great British victory. To be able, *during a match*, to gather a concert audience of ice-hockey *aficianados* is quite something, even if they do bring their own commentator.

Insects

Insects, whatever they may do to the performer, are a cause of hyper-anxiety to the audience, who can only sit helplessly, and watch the drama.

I remember a sultry afternoon in Darmstadt, when Yvonne Loriod was performing the *Vingt Regards sur l'Enfant Jésus* by Messiaen. Around xii-ième, a wasp sailed through the window. It made a few disdainful circles of the audience, then became hypnotised by Mlle Loriod, her hair, her face, and the way her fingers moved over the piano keys. The *Vingt Regards* are beautiful, but not brief, and tension began to build up.

Mlle Loriod made no concessions, bringing the greatest musical devotion to each phrase, and hurrying no tempo, however slow. As the work unfolded, the audience became more and more obsessed with imagined danger: sometimes Mlle Loriod and the wasp seemed to be making for the same note, figuration could be interpreted by the wasp as an attempt to frighten it away, a sudden chord as a brute attempt to wipe it out on the keyboard. At the end of xix-ième, the pitch of nerves was several ledger lines above the stave.

By a happy anticlimax, nothing happened. The wasp made a quick exit, frightened by the applause.

Although he was not in the same physical danger, **Lionel Salter** suffered from a multiplicity of tiny invaders. He was like the beleaguered hero of a Hitchcock film. It all took place in Aix-en-Provence:

> It was a hot, dark night, and seemingly nobody had foreseen what might happen when powerful arc-lights were switched on over the platform on which my partner and I were to play Bach violin sonatas. Attracted by the brightness, every fly, every mosquito, every bug, every insect of every kind in the South of France made a bee-line (sorry!) for

the illuminated area, covering our music, instruments, faces and hands. Every time my fingers tried to make contact with a key, they found the space pre-empted by winged creatures who got squashed in the process; and what with trying to brush the music clear of apparent notes that proved to be mobile, blowing insects off my glasses, shaking my hands free in the all too few rests Bach provides, *and* attempting to keep my mind on the music, these must have been very unusual performances.

In 1978, Martin Best was having tarantula trouble before his concert at Woollongong, New South Wales, as he has already described. He may not know that in the same year, on the other side of the continent in Perth, the soprano **Jane Manning** was battling with a fly in what must in many ways be the ultimate insect experience. Messiaen was again involved:

Early March, therefore boiling hot temperatures. A lunch-time recital in the University Chapel. Messiaen's *Poèmes pour Mi*. At an especially rapt and reverend passage of slow, poised music, the inevitable persistent Australian fly appeared (doors were open because of the heat).

I am totally attractive to flies, especially when perspiring: this one started to buzz round me, whizzing in circles nearer and nearer to my face. In the busier passages I managed a few adroit flicks of the hand, but it would not go away. Eventually, the music reached its most hushed and reverential phrase, during which the fly perched on my forehead, crawled down my nose, and, during a piano solo passage, settled on my upper lip at the moment I was bracing myself for a sudden vocal re-entry. To make more hand movements would clearly spoil the atmosphere.

Only the front few rows of the audience could see the reason for my fidgeting and it was already distracting the rest, so nothing could be done: while the front row watched in fascinated horror, I swiftly took my breath in through the mouth, sharply sucking the fly inwards, lizard-style, and, inevitably, swallowed it whole… and sang on – the only way of getting rid of it!

We know the importance of winged creatures to Messiaen as a composer, but this is ridiculous.

Intermezzo Bizarro

Sarah Walker

Many years ago, when I still sang the odd session as a professional chorister to keep the wolf from the door, I was asked to do some backing for a record of Christmas carols, bizarre enough perhaps on an August Saturday morning in the cavernous, distinctly *un*glamorous No. 1 Abbey Road – EMI's studios.

Adding to the incongruity of 'The First Noel' in eighty degrees of summer heat, was a fifteen foot high, splendidly decorated Christmas tree standing in one corner, where the publicity guys had obviously been doing some shots of the pop group who were the stars of the album.

A large, all-male (and, incidentally, very illustrious) session orchestra had been assembled, and I was one of only six or seven girls in the choir. At the end of the tea break I was the *only* girl in the studio, as I had stayed reading my book rather than fight my way to the coffee bar. Our 'fixer' came to me and asked if I would like to wait outside with the other girls as there was to be a short 'entertainment' for the band, arranged by the pop group, consisting of a stripper! "Pull the other one!" said I. Gullible I may be, but not stupid – and anyway I'd never seen a stripper.

Sure enough, the Tannoy system suddenly blared out suitably moody, 'big band' revue music, and in through the main studio doors 'shimmied' a hennaed redhead dressed in a shiny emerald-green satin number, and brandishing two enormous emerald-green ostrich feather fans! She went through her routine, casting off gloves, stockings, etc., even 'mingling' a little with the boys in the band, although, unfortunately for the brass and percussion sitting at the back (undoubtedly the most appreciative of her audience), she stayed mainly among the violins and cellos. One of our most distinguished cellists, a member of a renowned chamber ensemble, was persuaded to unzip her dress, which he did with elegant, if somewhat reluctant grace!

The young lady then mounted a small, hastily assembled dais, and completed her act – G string et al – and made her exit amid much flourishing of fans. She was given a warm, if not quite rapturous, ovation and the session continued as normal.

The punchline for Miss Walker came that evening, when she was standing in the wings at the Coliseum, waiting for her entry in Act III of *Rosenkavalier*. She suddenly heard an indignant yell of "Ask her – she was there!" It was the clarinettist in the off-stage band, goaded by disbelief among his colleagues.

Other Distractions

Other distractions from the natural world, besides insects, manifest themselves from time to time.

There was the Swedish girl flasher in the front row, who flashed at **Martin Best,** as he was singing an 18th-century song of great delicacy. Faced with her, he did not know where to look, so he says.

Nature in the raw is not always so kind, alas.

Angry gods seemed to be hurling themselves at the Academy of St Martin-in-the-Fields when they were playing in the Herodes Atticus amphitheatre at Athens. Appropriately enough, the work was The Four Seasons. Survivor **Iona Brown** sketches a wild and dreadful picture of the orchestra trying to play in a gale, the audience sitting on wet cushions, with their music attached to the stands with clothes-pegs. The wind was so strong it blew the bow off the strings of Miss Brown's violin, and her hair over her face, so that she could not see. To complete the scene, bats were flying about all over the place.

Not unlike this, was the drama in an outdoor concert hall near Melbourne. **Christopher Martin** was playing the solo viola in Berlioz's *Harold in Italy*. It is a stormy work. Berlioz describes the brass as seeming to "vomit curses and answer prayer with blasphemy". The brass might well have vomited a few, because a real storm blew up, carrying ash with it from the forest fires of that year. There was no question of fixing the music on the stands with clothes-pegs, or anything else. The stands themselves blew over, and the music scattered. Slowly, still playing, the orchestra disappeared from view in a storm cloud of ash. The concert was abandoned.

Performing out of doors is always a hazard. Even if you avoid a distraction as all-embracing as that, you can be thrown out of gear by a simple progression from the sublime to the ridiculous. There was, for instance, the lake-side performance of *Dido and Aeneas*, which **John Eliot Gardiner** was conducting. All went well until Dido's Lament, when **Felicity Palmer** suddenly found she was singing to the accompaniment of quacking ducks.

Indoors, you may be spared the direct intervention of the natural world, but if something happens in the way of a noise off in what should be a peaceful ambience, it comes in full focus, with the added element of shock. The quieter the music, of course, then the greater the shock. The Academy of St Martin-in-the-Fields were performing Samuel Barber's Adagio for strings, and had reached that moment towards the end, technically not the easiest to bring off, when there is a climax on a triple forte held chord in the high register, followed by a passage to be played as softly as humanly possible, which leads in to the final section. It is a moment of great beauty.

The orchestra successfully made the cross, and were following Iona Brown in a celestial pianissimo, when a hideous sustained squeal started in the auditorium, as if some demon in hell had stood up to make a point of order. It drowned Mr Barber's bridge passage, and seemed set to go on for ever – until a lady in the front row of the audience shamefacedly put a hand to the top of her dress, and turned down the volume of her hearing aid.

(If we are going to play this work again, listeners are kindly requested not to adjust their sets each time the music goes soft. It will get loud again by itself.)

A rather poignant distraction was the wandering platypus at the opening of the Sydney Opera House. **Sir Charles Mackerras** was conducting *The Magic Flute* for this occasion. John Copley had the idea that, when Tamino plays the flute to the animals, they should be Australian animals – koalas, etc. The little platypus boy somehow got separated from the herd, and went the wrong way. Like one of those Disney animals that go astray, he crawled off on his own, but could not see he was heading straight for the orchestra pit. Under the horrified eyes of Sir Charles and the audience, he got nearer and nearer the edge. Suddenly, a stage hand in modern jeans entered in a rush to scoop him up, and dragged him into the wings. It might have broken the magic, but just as well. Enough has already fallen into the orchestra pit.

Opera is, of course, the main field for visual distractions. **Katharine Hart** was playing the important viola part in Britten's *The Turn Of The Screw* for a production by the Piccola Scala at Como. It was a performance odd to the eye. As the drama became more intense and strange, so the scenery and projection system got in more and more of a muddle. It reached a climax of incongruity when the lights rose on the eerie churchyard scene. The audience was startled to find almost the entire foreground occupied by a large double bed. Clearly Salvador Dali had been passing round the honeymoon pictures.

Another intriguing visual happening was at a London performance of Verdi's *Un Ballo in Maschera*, remembered by **Richard Nunn:**

> Act Three has a dramatic moment with the betrayed husband, in his study, about to draw lots with two conspirators as to which of them is going to kill his wife's lover. The wife enters upon the scene accidentally, on a rather frivolous errand, and is grimly made to stay, and draw the lucky name herself.
>
> The effect was rather spoiled on this particular night by the soprano, misdirected by the stage staff, making her entrance through the fireplace.
>
> It does not help that Verdi stipulated a *little* fireplace (un caminetto), nor that the first line she had to sing after that extraordinary entrance was "Oscar is here with an invitation from the Count." In the circumstances, one cannot think of a more fatuous remark.

Usually you can get one type of distraction, animal, visual, or mechanical in an evening, but if you get all three in succession, and furthermore have written the work yourself and are conducting it – that amounts to surfeit. **Karlheinz Stockhausen** must have felt that, in this case, as one exquisite disruption followed another on a Florentine summer night:

4 July 1980. First of four *Sirius* performances in Chiostro Santa Croce, Florence, 10 pm. Phantastic preparation, place, beautiful night, completely full, wonderful public (nobody smoked, because I had personally asked all the smoking Italians to stop smoking); everything harmonious, perfect.

A few minutes after the mysterious beginning, a loud noise, and the appearance of a gigantic dog running into the cloister, sniffing at people, barking. I was on 180 degrees, not being able to decide if I should stop or continue. About two minutes of the performance completely spoiled, then a crowd of people got control of the dog and led him out.

About half an hour later, suddenly a stroke, and the electricity was gone: 8-channel machine (electronic music), microphones, speakers, lights: everything stopped. It happened to be a perfect spot, where the music at the end of the season *Libra* faded out in soft noises of winds.

Pitch dark! Noises, running, shouting, waiting. After several minutes the electricity came back – the Italians had used an electric plug which was completely overcharged, and by chance they found another (with flashlights, in a more distant room), which was functioning.

'*Ende gut _ alles gut!*'

We finally come to the inside job – the distraction caused by your own colleague in performance. This is perhaps the hardest to bear. Duo work implies a certain mutual supportiveness, and also considerable concentration. This is impaired if your partner erupts into Sicilian passion on the concert platform. An extreme example? It happened to **Sir Peter Pears:**

In the later forties, I was from time to time engaged by my agent, Ibbs and Tillett, to take part in concerts in Wales, put on by Welsh male-voice groups (or parties!). Often a quartet of soloists were engaged, and we were required to sing duets, or sometimes a trio or a quartet as well as solos.

On one such occasion, in the early days, I was asked to sing with a very famous soprano heavyweight who had spent her entire career on the stage, and when it came to exchanging suggestions for a duet to sing together, our repertoire failed to overlap. I finally agreed to learn one of her choosing, and plumped for *Cavalleria Rusticana*, where the tenor spends his time rejecting the enraged soprano.

I went along and got a copy from Ascherberg, Hopwood and Crew, and learnt it up adequately, though I didn't dare think of singing it by heart. We met in Wales, and the rehearsal went smoothly and without incident.

In the evening, however, what was my astonishment but to find that during the very short piano introduction, Santuzza had disappeared from my side. A minute later, I felt her charging across the stage with a "Stay, Turiddu!", and my arm was grasped in a grip of iron. I was most embarrassed and ashamed, because I needed my score to sing from, and in any case would not have known the correct procedure, never having seen the opera, let alone sung in it. We carried on rather onesidedly, and I found her before long on her knees at my side, more and more aware of my own inadequacy.

We finished together, to my huge relief. And I managed to do better with an unaccompanied song in the other half of the concert.

But I shall never forget that terrible duet. I shall never feel the same about 'Cav'.

Mascara and Mendelssohn

Iona Brown was playing the Mendelssohn Violin Concerto, when her mascara got in her eye. The work affords few possibilities of being able to put that sort of thing right. Even in the breaks between movements, you can do little except smear it over the rest of your face. So Miss Brown played on, hardly able to see, and with black tears pouring down her cheeks throughout the concert.

The audience must have wondered at such an intense emotional reaction to a work which really seems rather jolly. One hopes there was a little unease in critical or *Musikwissenschaftler* circles that perhaps Miss Brown had discovered something they had been missing all this time.

No Performance

I took my harp to a party, but nobody asked me to play, goes the song. **Sidonie Goossens** has a variation to that. She had brought her harp along, but the last thing she wanted was to be asked to play. It was in 1940, when the BBC Symphony Orchestra was stationed in Bristol, and she sought divine intervention on the matter.

> I was to play some solos at an afternoon broadcast with Billy Ternant's Orchestra, and I felt even more nervous than usual. After the opening selections, when I was waiting to put my harp into position, I found myself praying for an air raid warning, which would cancel the concert and send us all to the shelters. As if I had rubbed Aladdin's lamp, the sirens sounded, and we went to the shelters. That time, there was no air raid, but, a month later, Bristol was blitzed, and my punishment came. I lost everything but my harp. It was safe in the studio where I had said that prayer.

There is a meaning to this story. It reminds us, first, of the importance that is attached to the harp in celestial circles. Second, it makes clear that the Divine Impresario was not going to allow any more of this kind of thing from Miss Goossens. As a result, she remained Principal Harpist of the BBC Symphony Orchestra for another forty-two years, a joy for us all.

Oddly enough, the celesta does not seem to be taken so seriously in heaven. One might even say that a rather cynical attitude is adopted to it up there. **Betty Matthews,** when she was orchestral pianist with the Bournemouth Symphony Orchestra, was pressed into service at the last minute to play this instrument in Ravel's *Daphnis and Chloe* under a conductor of considerable renown. It was again in Bristol.

There are very few entries for the celesta, and there is much counting of bars, and listening for inaudible cues. I was never much good at 5/4 time. I missed every cue, did not play a single note, collected my money and got into the coach to go home. The conductor never noticed!

In that case, it is hardly worth writing for the thing. We take the hint.

Opera

If we add to the published cornucopia of operatic mishaps a few of our own, it is with no apology – rather the reverse. After all, they happened to our contributors.

There is a special fascination about things getting out of hand on the stage. They certainly did for **Nancy Evans** in the key scene of Britten's *The Rape of Lucretia:*

> The most awkward of my operatic memories occurred during a performance in 1947. I was Lucretia, and Otakar Kraus, Tarquinius.
>
> At the crucial moment in the rape scene, he leapt on to my bed, dagger held high, and there *should* have been a blackout, while the dramatic 'rape music' happened in the orchestra.
>
> But in full light, with the conductor looking horrified, Otto landed on top of me; there was much struggling and heavy breathing, and panic on my part, because I had only the 'rape music' for my quick change for the following scene. I tried to escape and run, but Otto held me down and said "Keep still", while I muttered "My quick change!" After an eternity the merciful blackout happened.
>
> I tore off, and just managed my entrance: I was supposed to be drained of emotion with shock – actually I was rather breathless. Otto's part was over, so he hadn't any problem: he came to my dressing-room afterwards and said very sweetly "I'm sorry darling, but I *had* to go on!"

The conductor, whose brief it is to keep everything together, and, of course, produce the perfect performance, can do little to help if things break down in the production department. He cannot leap over the pit, and if he could, it would be unfair to leave his stalwarts, sawing and blowing away down there. He becomes the captain of a ship in which there is no communication between the bridge and the engine room. (One well-known conductor, faced with a crisis of others' making, tried to buzz the stage director, only to be told by the switchboard that there was a performance going on.)

Sir Charles Mackerras, who has conducted more operas than most, has on several occasions had to endure the shuddering of ship meeting rock, without being able to do anything about it.

A special horror has been the non-happening of happenings carefully calculated by the composer (and his librettist of course) as of special dramatic effect. In Paris, for instance, the trombones did not come in when the Statue awesomely accepts Don Giovanni's invitation to dine with him. Mozart would have been furious. If he still uses the kind of language ascribed to him in a recent play made into a film, a four-letter word or two will have descended from heaven, and with far more reason.

Stage bands have been another hazard for Sir Charles. Opera composers love them, on and off stage, as an extra dimension. Sometimes they are more than an extra dimension, and part of the drama itself. Then, if they do not come in, it is complete disaster. The end of the second act of *La Bohème* depends on a military band marching into the square, and sweeping everyone off in its wake, just before the curtain. If it does not appear, nothing makes any more sense. As you will also have missed the build-up (the sound of the band coming nearer) it will make even less sense. What will happen?

People will have been rushing on stage. The crowd will part expectantly, for something, but in fact for nothing, and, after a few pizzicato chords, the orchestra will dry up. There is no music for anybody to play; the band is supposed to have taken over. There will be silence, the more embarrassing the longer it lasts. The band may be locked in the canteen, but we cannot leave things suspended like this; somehow the show must go on. It will be like a maniac madrigal.

The chorus will point joyfully into air, and sing "There he is, the drum major." They will probably point in different directions – it is difficult to gauge where a non-existent drum major

The big bass drum

has arrived at any given moment. They may even point across a void, at each other. But, as they are singing unaccompanied, it will be clear from the words that they have gone mad.

The principal singers will look on with detachment at first (Musetta is trying to make love to Marcello with only one shoe), then an unexpected burst from the orchestra – which dies in its tracks – will give them a bad attack of drum major, themselves. They will leap to their feet, singing "Hurry! Hurry! Hurry!" and join the hallucinated chorus, which now cannot wait to get off the stage. Making ridiculous marching movements, and singing (unaccompanied of course) at the tops of their voices, principals and chorus exeunt *en masse*, and it is just as well. Musetta has been hoisted onto somebody's shoulders, so that she can see better, whatever there is to see.

Small wonder that the only one left behind, who has to pick up the bill at the café Momus, slumps into a chair, *stupefatto*. I do not know what Sir Charles could have been feeling.

For the same kind of reason, Sir Charles had to witness the ruination of the end of *Carmen*, helpless at the helm. Here, the off-stage band, playing fortissimo, provides the festive atmosphere inside the bull-ring, while the terminal drama between Carmen and Don José is being enacted outside it.

Should the band not come in (and it didn't), Bizet's whole structure collapses. Gone is the dramatic irony, gone is the catchy tune everybody is waiting for, gone is the moment when Don José draws his knife on Carmen to a fanfare off stage. Pretty well everything is gone. Never mind, in only another twenty-three bars you can go too. Be careful where you choose, though. The band might be there.

Act Two of *The Marriage of Figaro* revolves round a door that is locked. Sir Charles conducted a performance on a stage which had a tilt. It was on tour at Wolverhampton. With the stage listing to starboard, there was no question of the door being 'locked' – it would not even remain closed. A few seconds, perhaps, of being shut, and it would gently swing open. Not all the furtive efforts of Susanna and the Countess to give it a quick shut as they flitted about the stage were of any avail. Nor was a dramatic dash from the wings by the stage manager. Whatever anyone did, the door would wearily droop open again.

It would be churlish to charge Mozart and da Ponte for not foreseeing this situation. Mozart might not have heard of Wolverhampton. Nevertheless, they bequeath an inescapable quandary, because the libretto is full of references to that damn door. The jealous Count: "Why is the door locked?" "Open the door!" "I mean to see who is behind that door!" "Where's the key, ma'am?" "Will you open the door, or must I?" "Then you refuse to open the door?" (Giggles start) "Very well, I'll fetch tools and break it down myself!" (That brings the house down), then Susanna: "Be quick, unlock the door now," etc. etc.

By this time, probably the Count himself is trying to keep it shut. Freudians in the audience would be interested.

If Sir Charles found a stage on a tilt, **Roger Norrington** found one that was even more threatening.

In 1980, the Theatre Royal, Bath, was in poor shape. When Mr Norrington arrived one autumn day to rehearse Verdi's *Falstaff* for that evening, the stage and the stage staff were in complete disarray. The staff had been hanging the scenery for the first act, when loud creakings emanated from the dilapidated structure, and pieces of wood and stone started falling on the stage. The theatre surveyor had ordered the scenery to be taken down forthwith, and forbidden the stage to be used. It was now two hours before the performance. The situation could fairly be described as a crisis.

Never in several years of touring had Kent Opera cancelled a performance, and Mr Norrington refused to be put off by the rather discouraging look of things. All were determined to do something to make an evening. They rang the surveyor for permission to use the first few feet of the stage, in front of the curtain. This was granted; presumably less masonry would fall on their heads there. They decided that, this way, they could give a concert performance at least, but then came another snag. The lead singer, who was to play Falstaff, had gone down with flu, and would not be singing that night.

Lesser men and women would have given up at that point, quite understandably thinking they were just not meant to give that performance. Not, though, Mr Norrington and Kent Opera. As if this double misfortune was the crack of a starting pistol, they resolved not only to go ahead, but, because they were an opera company, to give their performance in costume, despite every difficulty. There was no time for any kind of rehearsal, and one hour left before the audience arrived – an hour spent in people working out, by themselves and with each other, how to present an extremely mouvementé opera such as *Falstaff* on what amounted to a rather small raft.

The company was showing a game spirit; now it was a test of character for the audience. Roger Norrington spoke in front of the curtain, to a full house that as yet knew nothing.

I explained the twin problems of architecture and lead singer, and offered anyone, who wished, their money back. About two dozen purists left in disappointment, but the rest of the house stayed, perhaps mostly out of curiosity, to see what they must have thought would be a disaster. In the event, the evening was perhaps one of the most exciting performances of *Falstaff* I have ever conducted. We were on our metal to give our loyal audience a good show, and I think they got much more than they expected. Singers and orchestra, almost on top of each other in the cramped conditions, gave a tremendous account of the piece, and the audience seemed overjoyed. But it had been a very very near thing.

For the old Theatre Royal, it was the last thing. It closed for two years. Superbly refurbished from top to bottom, anyone is safe in it now. It is a relief to present one opera story with a happy ending.

Orchestral Interlude

If you are fighting a duel, and you get your sword stuck in its scabbard you look rather silly, to say the least. Transformed and elevated to the musical plane, this is what happened to one of the percussion players of the City of Birmingham Symphony Orchestra in a performance of Tchaikovsky's *Romeo and Juliet Overture* under George Weldon.

It is up to the cymbal player to depict the sword-play between Montagues and Capulets in a series of syncopated clashes, striking his two cymbals together in what should be an off-centre brushing movement. Unfortunately, a somewhat inexperienced Capulet (or Montague) was engaged on this occasion. On the last of his first round of clashes, he somehow got the cymbals precisely aligned face to face, so that they stuck together in a vacuum. Nothing could prise them apart. His Laocoön struggles

In affectionate memory of Gerard

to get back into the fight were spotted by the audience – the percussion section in Birmingham Town Hall sits high left, clearly visible to all – and the inevitable hilarity rapidly spread into the rest of the orchestra. Romeo and Juliet would have been much happier if there had been a bit of that humour in Verona as well, and the fighting had dissolved now and again into laughter. But then there wouldn't have been a story, nor this despatch from **Beresford King-Smith,** the orchestra's deputy general manager.

Proceeding north-east, we find another percussion player, this time in amazing trouble.

Untoward Events in Newcastle

Sir John Pritchard was conducting the Royal Liverpool Philharmonic Orchestra in one of their regular visits to Newcastle, and the main work in the programme was the *Symphonie Fantastique* of Berlioz. In the last movement Sir John likes to have the all-important theme of the *Dies irae*, played on large tubular bells, amplified and performed offstage to give an effect of great resonance and power.

On this occasion a new recruit to the percussion section, rejoicing in the name of Muddiman, was entrusted with the tubular bell part and was duly rehearsed in the afternoon stationed in front of a microphone just outside the left-hand entrance to the platform, immediately behind the first violins. The door had to be opened a few inches so that the player could see the beat, and at the rehearsal all went well.

In the evening, Sir John recalls that he had a feeling of nervousness as the great moment approached, but glancing to his left he noticed the door had been slightly opened and presumed Mr Muddiman was poised for action. At the actual point of entry, when the rest of the orchestra is silent, Sir John gave a vigorous beat in the direction of the open door – nothing. Now the pulse of the music cannot be halted here and important violin entrances *must* be made correctly, or endless confusion will follow. Hesitating only a moment, the conductor gestured even more vigorously at the door, and with cataclysmic effect the great theme rang out, enormously inflated by the amplifications and several bars wrong! At this point Mr Muddiman with all these decibels at his disposal, had more control over the proceedings than Sir John, as was proved when in his elation he produced startling variations of rhythm so that the 'Dies Irae' became definitely jazzy. Meanwhile the rest of the orchestra were skeetering about desperately trying to catch up with the bells, and disaster seemed imminent.

Sir John, usually cool in a crisis but now under extreme pressure, decided on decisive action and speaking to a trusted deputy leader at the front of the violins said "Stop him, Tom," and the gentleman named put down his violin and started towards the door. Now by ill chance that day there were no less than *three* 'Toms' in the violins and the audience was surprised to see *all three* musicians suddenly rise from their places. One of these gentlemen had the additional misfortune, scarcely to be believed, to catch the fly of his trousers in the sweeping bow of a colleague, with the result that he suddenly bent double in alarm and confusion.

The climax of the episode arrived as the original 'Tom' reached Mr Muddiman and restrained him, whereupon the audience was startled to hear, hugely amplified around the hall, Mr Muddiman's voice, "The f ******* door closed..."

Aria Schifosa: 'The Retreat from Maida Vale'

Synopsis: **Gareth Morris** sings of the Philharmonia Orchestra in a nasty mess. During a pleasant rehearsal (sic) at the BBC studios in Maida Vale, the air-conditioning apparatus has suddenly reversed itself with no warning. "Instead of extracting the impurities in the air being breathed by the fastidious members of the Philharmonia Orchestra, it blew clouds of filthy soot-like dust into the room." The climax comes in an excited Cabaletta, one minute later, describing the orchestra as "eighty chimney-sweeps rushing home to hot baths and the dry-cleaners".

Page Turners

Turning the page is so vital and dangerous a branch of music-making, that it is strange there should be no training for it. No course exists, at the end of which one emerges a FLIP (Fellow-Licentiate of the Institute of Page Turners), and knows that after a long apprenticeship one is safe at last. The system as it is, is wildly *ad hoc*, and puts page turners into two categories – volunteers and conscripts.

The conscripts are the depressives. They know they have been chosen because there was no one else in sight who looked as if they could tell a crotchet from a crowbar – chosen, in fact, with less care than one would choose a lemon at a supermarket. Deeply aware of their own inadequacy and the range of catastrophes they could cause, they suffer from concert nerves vastly exceeding anything the player might be going through.

The volunteer is of course the manic. Super-confident, he is blessed with that rare gift of being able to follow music at twice the speed it is being played, and as a result starts to turn the page before the player has even got half-way down it. Tears follow. The player, with a whole chunk of music rapidly vanishing before his eyes, angrily tries to wrench the page back again. A deadly game starts, which could last the whole piece.

To be fair, the page turner is often as much sinned against as sinning. There is nothing more disconcerting, for instance, than finding pages that have stuck themselves together, and having somehow to disengage them while the show is going relentlessly on. Worse still, if the pages have been stuck together *deliberately* and no one has told you. Your efforts to part them then look like extraordinarily ill-timed nosiness.

There was no way **John Cruft,** turning over at a concert of new music, could possibly know that a rather fat page 5 was *meant* to be followed by page 9, because the composer had been at the glue-pot and had not changed the page numbers. Mr Cruft's efforts to diagnose the ailment in mid-stream received a rather nasty reaction from the pianist.

Despite everything, the system does work oddly well. Page turning is a delicate art, however, and it is an advantage to have two hands available for the job, – one to turn the pages, the other to steady the rest of the music, or, if necessary, the player. **Gillian Weir,** on a whistle-stop tour in foreign parts, was not encouraged when told she was going to have a page turner who was wonderful, but had only one arm. She thought this was an example of the local humour, but it was not.

> When the organ malfunctioned, as I knew it would, he stood there wringing his hand softly, while I had to summon the organ builder on to the stage.

This does not mean, we hasten to assure the reader, that Miss Weir expected the page turner to mend the organ himself – especially single-handed – but to go for help.

Miss Weir must be turner-prone. On another occasion, at Art-staff, Switzerland, the page turner knocked the music on to the pedal. She and he were conversing in French, and

> when he tried to extricate the page from between my feet while I continued to play, I must say I found a completely new fluency in the language I didn't know I had, plus an unusual vocabulary.
>
> However, he did get it back on the music desk quite safely. Unfortunately upside down.

Gillian Weir's headiest encounter with a page turner was at her début.

> Perhaps I've been doomed with page turners ever since I first played in London in public at my very first recital, which was in the big Methodist Central Hall.
>
> I had again, a very nervous page turner, who had been told he must not drop the music, especially coming on stage.
>
> I forgot to warn him of stage procedure: I advanced to the front of the stage wearing a rather beautiful dress with a

train. He advanced, worriedly looking at the music, and – still holding it very tightly – fell over my train, and fell over me as I turned to bow to the audience. Our heads met with a tremendous ringing crash, that went right through the hall!

The performance was a great success, no doubt because the audience was still happily laughing, and inclined to cheer anything. But it killed a beautiful friendship.

In fairness to page turners it must be said that quite the most extraordinary things happen to Miss Weir. They need to be men of unusual resource. On one occasion, she gave the swell pedal a big heave in the middle of an exciting piece, and found herself in the music cupboard. She screamed at the page turner "Push me, push me in again!"

If I might contribute a story of my own:

I was asked to turn over for **George Malcolm** at a recital he gave with **Elaine Shaffer** at the Pollensa Festival, Majorca. The concert took place in the beautiful open cloisters, which also happened to be the local Red Cross station.

I was suffering from terrible pre-concert nerves, with visions of my dashing the music to the floor, and ruining the concert. That was a conceit, as there would be little I could do which would upset the performance of two such artists.

The audience, sun-tanned in their white tuxedos and glamorous dresses were filing expensively into the open auditorium. Seeing the state I was in, George Malcolm said "Come with me. I want to show you something."

Behind one door, Elaine Shaffer was practising brilliant arpeggios on the flute. Behind the next door, through which George Malcolm showed me, was a dead woman lying in state, surrounded by her keening family.

That encounter with the ultimate reality did the trick. I turned over with assurance, and a certain detachment.

All the same, the contrast between what we and the audience were doing, and what was happening a few feet to the left, is something I shall not forget easily.

Pianos

We are told that there was nothing the late Franz Liszt enjoyed more, than coming across a really grotty piano when he was on tour. One finds that hard to believe. It is more likely that it was a contributory factor to his eventually becoming an Abbé.

Some remarkable pianos make their appearances elsewhere in this book, more or less *en passant*. Here are a few, which in their own right wrought disaster, or near-disaster on the victim-player.

Roger Vignoles writes; "The instruments that sometimes go by this description" (he refers to the genus 'piano'), "can be a severe test of one's adaptability and sang-froid. The one in question was the property of a music club in South London, who should have known better."

The tenor Neil Jenkins and I were performing Schumann's *Dichterliebe*. In rehearsal, I had discovered a problem with the sustaining pedal; the connecting rod between pedal and dampers was chipped, as a result of which the damper-bar had slipped off. All that emerged from the piano was an ugly, dry staccato hardly appropriate to Schumann's romantic lyricism.

Fortunately, it did not take a great deal of engineering skill to re-align the mechanism, and restore a semblance of singing tone to the instrument. So, with a mental note to treat it gently we launched into the performance.

All went swimmingly until '*Ich grolle nicht*'. This is the one song that it is impossible to play in a tentative fashion, and, sure enough, with the final truculent chord came an ominous thud. My worst fears were confirmed by the very next song, '*Und wuessten's die Blumen, die kleinen*'. What should have sounded like a shower of fragrant blossoms, was reduced to the brittle clatter of hailstones.

There was nothing for it but to announce a break in the

proceedings. "Ladies and gentlemen, I regret to say I shall have to carry out running repairs." Neil vanished to a side passage, while I treated the audience to the spectacle of their pianist prostrate beneath the instrument like a motor mechanic in full evening dress, nothing sartorial having been forgotten on this occasion.

We continued, kid gloves well to the fore, to the end of the cycle, and it is a tribute to my partner's presence of mind that he got through without a single mistake in music or words.

Then there was the piano at Ajmer, India, which became the subject of both Woman's Hour and Pick of the Week. It could well have been Steinway's Opus One, at least so it appeared to **Rodney Slatford**, on a world tour with the pianist **Clifford Lee**. The local tuner, Mr Mozart by name, had been fetched from the neighbouring village especially to tune it for the concert.

Mr Mozart was the best Peter Sellers material. He started by systematically tuning all the B flats to B natural, then pronounced the instrument "very badly out of tune indeed".
This left Mr Slatford in something of a quandary.

Not wishing to seem impolite, I left Mr Mozart to his business. Returning to check the piano an hour before we played, my worst fears were confirmed. The middle octaves were totally devoid of B flats, but on the other hand these vital notes gradually returned as one ascended or descended the keyboard. The effect of Rossini's *Cenerentola* overture (in F) was devastatingly comic.

I had to re-tune the piano before it could be used. I managed with only limited success.

John McCabe met two interesting pianos, the second homicidal:

The greatest problem for pianists is that they seldom know what calibre of instrument they are going to be given.

I came across what still qualifies as the worst of my experience in a castle in Wales, where I was playing, amongst other things, the complete *Miroirs* of Ravel, which need a first-rate instrument to come off properly. One of the movements is the *Alborado del Gracioso*, notoriously difficult in general anyway, but in particular for its repeated notes, which need a piano with a lightish action, and for its glissandi in thirds and fourths.

The repeated notes were, on this occasion, no problem. When, with great vigour, I launched into the first of the glissandi, however, all the ivories came off the keys, in a magnificent but inappropriate cascade of white.

Number Two was beautiful and beckoning. How many men have been lured to their doom in this way! Mr McCabe was on a tour in Ayrshire, with the hornist **Ifor James:**

The piano, to my great relief, was a splendid, full-size Steinway grand. (Beware! Ed.)

The programme contained, among numerous other things, the Mozart Concert Rondo for horn and piano, followed by a work of mine called *The Castle of Arianrhod*, which I was due to introduce while Ifor indulged in the hornist's traditional pastime of emptying out the 'condensation'.

We reached the end of the Mozart in fine style, played the final chords with gusto, and I stood up to take a bow. By doing this, I managed to escape decapitation, because the nearest hinge on the piano lid had apparently come loose, and as I stood up, the lid swept past my left ear to the floor. Naturally, the floor was wooden, and in the horrified silence which accompanied this spectacle, the only sound to be heard was of this superb piano lid clattering to rest.

A moment's pause, and we decided to get on with the show, so I began to introduce my work.

Half-way through the introduction, my colleague suddenly developed hysterics, whereupon I joined him, whereupon hysteria began to spread through the audience. Order was eventually restored, but I shall never forget that hall ringing to the sound of hysterical laughter.

I was under the impression that the concert was being recorded on video for local educational authorities. A few years later, I bumped into one of the organisers in London, and he assured me it had not been.

A pity – I would like to have seen that moment again.

Yes, and what a great idea for video. Look, there's this killer piano, haunting the Castle of Arianrhod. It starts to move, slowly at first...

We cannot resist ending with what must be one of the greatest piano stories of the century. We can make no claim that it is a 'scoop' for this book; it is a review by Kenneth Langbell in the *Bangkok Post*, which was made available to the Western world by Martin Bernheimer of the *Los Angeles Times*. Headed A HUMID RECITAL STIRS BANGKOK, it goes as follows:

> The recital last evening in the chamber music room of the Erawan Hotel by US pianist Myron Kropp, the first appearance of Mr Kropp in Bangkok, can only be described by this reviewer and those who witnessed Mr Kropp's performance as one of the most interesting experiences in a very long time.
>
> A hush fell over the room as Mr Kropp appeared from the right of the stage, attired in black formal evening wear with a small white poppy in his lapel. With sparse, sandy hair, a sallow complexion and a deceptively frail-looking frame, the man who has repopularised Johann Sebastian Bach approached the Baldwin Concert Grand, bowed to the audience and placed himself upon the stool.
>
> It might be appropriate to insert at this juncture that many pianists, including Mr Kropp, prefer a bench, maintaining that on a screw-type stool they sometimes find themselves turning sideways during a particularly expressive strain. There was a slight delay, in fact, as Mr Kropp left the stage briefly, apparently in search of a bench, but returned when informed there was none.
>
> As I have mentioned on several other occasions, the Baldwin Concert Grand, while basically a fine instrument, needs constant attention, particularly in a climate such as Bangkok's. This is even more true when the instrument is as old as the one provided in the chamber music room at the Erawan Hotel. In this humidity the felts which separate the white keys from the black tend to swell, causing an occasional key to stick, which apparently was the case last

evening with the D in the second octave.

During the 'raging storm' section of the D-minor Toccata and Fugue, Mr Kropp must be complimented for putting up with the awkward D. However, by the time the 'storm' was past and he had gotten into the Prelude and Fugue in D major, in which the second octave D plays a major role, Mr Kropp's patience was wearing thin.

Some who attended the performance later questioned whether the awkward key justified some of the language which was heard coming from the stage during softer passages of the fugue. However, one member of the audience, who had sent his children out of the room by the midway point of the Fugue, had a valid point when he commented over the music and extemporaneous remarks of Mr Kropp that the workman who greased the stool might have done better to use some of the grease on the second octave D. Indeed, Mr Kropp's stool had more than enough grease, and during one passage in which the music and lyrics both were particularly violent, Mr Kropp was turned completely round. Whereas before his remarks had been aimed largely at the piano and were therefore somewhat muted, to his surprise and that of those in the chamber music room he found himself addressing directly to the audience.

But such things do happen, and the person who began to laugh deserves to be severely reprimanded for this undignified behaviour. Unfortunately, laughter is contagious, and by the time it had subsided and the audience had regained its composure Mr Kropp appeared to be somewhat shaken. Nevertheless he swivelled himself back into position facing the piano and, leaving the D major Fugue unfinished, commenced on the Fantasia and Fugue in G minor.

Why the concert grand piano's G key in the third octave chose that particular time to begin sticking I hesitate to guess. However, it is certainly safe to say that Mr Kropp himself did nothing to help matters when he began using his feet to kick the lower portion of the piano instead of operating the pedals as is generally done.

Possibly it was this jarring, or the un-Bach-like hammering to which the sticking keyboard was being subjected.

Something caused the right front leg of the piano to buckle slightly inward, leaving the entire instrument listing at approximately a 35-degree angle from that which is normal. A gasp went up from the audience, for if the piano had actually fallen, several of Mr Kropp's toes, if not both his feet, would surely have been broken.

It was with a sigh of relief, therefore, that the audience saw Mr Kropp slowly rise from his stool and leave the stage. A few men in the back of the room began clapping, and when Mr Kropp reappeared a moment later it seemed he was responding to the ovation. Apparently, however, he had left to get the red-handled fire axe which was hung backstage in case of fire, for that was what he had in his hand.

My first reaction at seeing Mr Kropp begin to chop at the left leg of the grand piano was that he was attempting to make it tilt at the same angle as the right leg, and thereby correct the list. However, when the weakened legs finally

collapsed altogether with a great crash and Mr Kropp continued to chop, it became obvious to all that he had no
intention of going on with the concert.

The ushers, who had heard the snapping of piano wires
and splintering of sounding board from the dining-room,
came rushing in and, with the help of the hotel manager,
two Indian watchmen and a passing police corporal, finally
succeeded in disarming Mr Kropp and dragging him off the
stage.

Tours

Tours go wrong, and the further from home the more so. We can cope with our own muddles, but those of other countries are based on thought patterns which – one hates to say it – sometimes seem so foreign as to approach the lunatic. The late **André Tchaikowsky,** for instance, when on a South American tour received a telegram from the impresario saying "Please proceed São Paolo. Concert yesterday".

Much can happen on tour, and it has to our contributors. On the simplest level, one can *lose* things, such as:

All the Instruments of the Orchestra

The whole lot, belonging to the London Symphony Orchestra, disappeared between Boston Airport and Symphony Hall the night before the first concert of a big tour. Next morning, they were recovered at gun-point in a motel.

The explanation is rather complicated, and **Gervase de Peyer** says there has to be a moral to it:

At the working end of the guns were the Massachusetts police, and at the wrong end were the two drivers of the truck carrying the instruments. The drivers were in bed. They had overslept, and were in a different motel to where they had been booked. They had been too tired to find the right one, and had only been discovered because an alert patrolman had spotted the rear end of the truck sticking out behind the building.

To bring the police in for something like this may seem excessive at first glance. United States law does not force you to go to bed in the motel where you are booked, tidy though it might be for everybody. (It is safe to say that any Administration which sought to bring in such a measure would be told to knock it off.) In this case, though, there was some justifiable panic. The drivers had not communicated with anyone (perhaps in their exhaustion they had even thought they were in the right place), – and in the morning had overslept, and not turned up at Symphony Hall with the instruments.

If they were fatigued, it was because they had driven non-stop from *Texas* to Boston Airport to pick up the instruments. They had done this because their truck had been hired in Texas, and in Texas because rents are cheaper down there than in Massachusetts.

It all comes down to money, then, and if there is a moral, it is for Heaven's sake don't try and save it if it means police in the bedroom.

Your Finger-tip

This is rare, thank God, but it happened to **Jane Manning** *en route* for a tour of Scotland. She severed hers in a loo door on the London-Edinburgh express.

Helpful fellow-musicians duly went back and found it still wedged in the hinge, while the guard pulled the communi-

cation cord and a special stop was made for me to be taken to hospital in Doncaster to have it stitched on. I reappeared that evening in Edinburgh for the first concert with a spectacular bandage – *Pierrot Lunaire* seemed a suitably bloodthirsty work to perform in that condition.

The real hero was the principal bassoonist with the Northern Sinfonia*, who was the actual bearer of my finger-tip – carrying it all the way through the restaurant car and the length of the train, to find me propped up in the guard's van. He has never forgotten the incident.

Nor, I imagine, has the restaurant car.

Your Freedom, because there is no bomb in your baggage

(A cautionary tale on a theme we shall meet again, of travelling about with any stringed instrument larger than a violin.)

Peter Carter, leader of the **Allegri String Quartet** tells his story:

The transportation of a cello is always a disaster area, and our trip to Canada in 1979 was fraught with problems. To start with, our air fares (Apex) were £243 each, and the quote for the cello was £476. Not being human, it did not qualify for an Apex fare. So we decided not to buy it a seat... Nevertheless, we still thought it worthwhile to try and persuade the airline to allow it on board, as opposed to the hold. This they frequently do if it is not a very full flight, and the supervisor is in a good mood and appreciates Bruno, our cellist's special brand of charm. It didn't work on the way out to Canada, but, after our Montreal concert, we were flying to Sudbury, which we understood to be the place most like the moon on earth – the astronauts go there to practise.

We arranged for a taxi to collect us at 5.30 am for the 7 am flight from Montreal. At 5 am he arrived in a panic, as there had been a blizzard in the night, and he expected trouble on the motorway to the airport. How right he was! The signposts were covered in snow, he couldn't tell which way to

---

*Michael Chapman, now with the Royal Philharmonic Orchestra.

go, got lost, broke goodness knows how many traffic laws trying to get on the right road, and eventually deposited us at the airport about 6.40 am. 'Charm' was not in abundance at the time.

Nevertheless we tried to persuade the baggage supervisor that there was room on the flight for a very special old valuable etc. cello. To our surprise, having pressed a few keys on the computer, he agreed there was. Things were looking up. Not for long, though. Security had other ideas. Back we got to the supervisor. "These security people think they own the place!" he explodes. Back to Security. "Cellos are not allowed on flights without tickets."

David and Pru (second violin and viola) have passed through security and gone on to the plane, my violin has disappeared through the x-ray machine, and Bruno and I seem to be at an impasse. Back again to the supervisor, this time with one of the security brigade. At the sight of him, the supervisor capitulates. "I didn't realise it was a cello: I thought it was a violin. I'm not up in classical instruments." "What do we do now?" I ask. "Send it in the hold?" The flight has closed – no way of sending anything in the hold. "Pay for a ticket?" There's a queue half a mile long for tickets. "Can you at least get me to the front of the queue?" (It's now 7 am). "It's too late. Your flight has left." Sure in my mind that he had just lost interest in our plight and was bluffing (he wasn't), I exploded: "Then you'd better bring it back. For all you know, there may be a bomb in my bags."

The supervisor disappeared. I found an air hostess, explained the predicament, was taken to the front of the queue, was about to pay for the ticket for the cello, when a Canadian Mounted Policeman, resplendent in Mountie uniform, put his hand on my shoulder. "Did you say there was a bomb on board that flight?" he asked. "Of course not," I said. "The possibility merely exists as far as the airline is concerned, if I check in my baggage and don't get on the flight myself." The flight, which had taxied to the end of the runway (an amazingly irresponsible act) was brought back, our bags removed, and I was arrested for committing a public mischief.

All this by 7.15 am. The previous evening, at a reception after the concert, we had met the British Consul. "If ever you need any help, just get in touch," he said as we parted. Little did he realise that at 7.30 the next morning, I would be calling him for help from the local prison.

Things went from bad to worse: the local prosecution decided to oppose bail as I was a foreigner, and if I wanted to plead 'Not Guilty' the first chance of a trial would be in July. It was now April. If I were to plead guilty and pay a fine or have a sentence, I would carry a criminal record for the rest of my life, and certainly wouldn't be allowed back in Canada (not that this latter point worried me particularly at the time). From worse to worser; the airline was going to sue me for several million dollars for the loss of the flight, as the delay meant that it never took off because the weather had deteriorated.

As I sat humiliated in prison, pinching myself in the vain hope that it was all a bad dream, the rest of the Quartet were frantically exploring all avenues to secure my release. David's brother-in-law is a QC in Toronto. He put us in touch with a QC in Montreal, who worked wonders. At my arraignment, and after I had spent a long and anxious night in prison, he persuaded the judge that I should be given bail to complete the tour, arranged for the trial to be held on the last day of the tour before our flight home, and then, wonder of wonders, discovered a technicality which meant there was no charge to answer, a point he could not disclose until the prosecution had rested its case at the trial. All this in face of much opposition from the prosecuting counsel, who seemed determined to obstruct in every possible way, even considering re-arresting me in order to change the charge. Again the QC charmed him into kinder ways, but not before I had been sent to hide in the Gents to avoid re-arrest.

All this cost legal fees of 1,500 dollars, half his normal fee as we were 'friends'. A seat for the cello would have been cheap at the price.

Travels With My Bass (*pace* Julian Lloyd Webber)
As shown in the last story, if you want to take one of the larger

instruments with you on the plane, you have to buy it a ticket. Convention sometimes decrees that you also give it a *name*. This can lead to ludicrous encounters with airport officials. **Barry Guy** arrived at Charles De Gaulle airport with a ticket for his double bass in the name of Mrs Guy. The man at the desk absolutely refused to believe that Mr Guy's enormous and strange-shaped companion could be his wife. Mr Guy agreed that it was indeed not his wife, but it was only a formality, and to the travel agent it seemed the best idea at the time. He lost the battle and had to buy another ticket – in the name of Mrs *Bass!*

Before handing over to Mr Guy to tell his story of manhandling his double bass in a nightmare dash across Berlin, we should let you know exactly what it was he was manhandling. It was the instrument in its hard case known as the 'coffin' which, as *The Guinness Book of Records* might say, is an unbelievable six feet nine inches in length.

In the East Berlin Underground, heading, late, for Tegal Airport in the West is Barry Guy:

It was a panic since we were well behind our schedule, so getting through the border at the Underground quickly was imperative. The inevitable happened... the large coffin proved attractive to the guards who opened everything up. Bass (in soft cover) out... bows examined... spare strings examined.. the foam within the case scrutinised... torch examining the inside of the instrument... Before me were my anxious musician friends who got through, and waited a few minutes before saying they would have to leave as their plane was 10 minutes before mine. They had done the journey before, and knew the ropes – me, no! I shouted to them to suggest directions – "Oh, take the U Bahn or S Bahn or something to the airport..." I waved them goodbye as my case was being examined.

The journey after this was horrible. I only had one thought in mind – get to Tegal. This was easier said than done, since I could not really understand the directions, or indeed knew which line to take. I knew that if I missed the flight I would seriously mess up my next engagement in England and have to pay a new fare without recompense.

For ages I climbed stairs, walked corridors and staggered with my load from place to place studying S Bahn and U Bahn on the way, realising slowly that time was running out. Eventually I found a line that said TEGAL. By this time I was reduced to throwing my bag down a flight of stairs ahead of me and lifting my coffin as if I were a wrestler fighting for the last round. Finally I found the line that said the magic word. Realising this and on hearing a train pull in, I once again threw my bag the whole flight of the stairs that spread before me, and manhandled my bass towards the stationary train. At the bottom of the stairs I picked up my bag, threw it in the open doors, and began to follow with my bass. The doors began to close. In a desperate effort I thrust my bass case between them and succeeded in obliging the guard to open them again, allowing me to drag the whole assemblage within the carriage. This scenario produced a howl from the assembled people within the carriage. I stood with my bass and bag like an invader that had transgressed every rule of the planet.

That moment gave me a moment of resolve for my efforts. I stood dripping but calm in the knowledge that at last I was on my way with precious few moments to lose. Studying the Underground map at some length during my momentary peace, I came to the nasty conclusion that Tegal was not Tegal the Airport. Tegal the Airport (if I remember correctly, St Marks Pltz) was a bus ride away. I felt somewhat weak mentally and physically at this point. The station arrived, and by good fortune two young girls offered to help me up the stairs with my bag, each taking one handle.

I thanked them and awaited the airport bus with thirty minutes left before the flight. I studied the journey time for this leg – ten minutes; I tried hailing cabs with roof racks, or estate cars, to no avail. Finally, fifteen minutes before the flight, the bus arrived.

I almost threw everything on in an effort to imply urgency, but managed to destroy the bus's roof light. The driver came to the rear to discuss the damage, but eventually seeing my somewhat advanced state of delirium, retreated to the driving position and headed for the airport. On arriving my happiness was without containment; I motored with my trolley to the nearest Pan Am counter, threw my ticket on the counter, only to be told after some examination that my flight was being handled at the opposite end of the check-in gates! At this point I thought I had blown it, but a rapid run found me at the gate with the gate closing. I pleaded, giving the Pan Am staff a short resumé of my past days, which resulted in me and my bass finally getting on the flight.

The relief was amazing – at last I was heading home. The only difficult part of the return was feeling embarrassed by sweating profusely and continually throughout the whole flight, which must have amazed the young lady next to me.

Next time I hope things will be different.

A week later Mr Guy was immovable, with three discs out.

Bass and Piano

Many players of the double bass probably consider their biggest musical disaster was the moment they decided to devote the remainder of their lives to the instrument. Apart from that there were a few minor happenings during a world tour **Rodney Slatford** gave in 1975, with his pianist, **Clifford Lee:**

All went well – relatively speaking – until we reached Australia, when the fingerboard came off the bass on a bank holiday Monday. The bridge fell down and the sound-post also collapsed, which added to my troubles. I managed these repairs with a bent coat-hanger, glue and some string, only to find that on arrival at our next venue the upright piano was a semitone flat, had no music rest, was propped up on a brick, and even had a mouse's nest in it.

But my pianist had other things on his mind. He had heard my schools patter during countless lecture-recitals, so I was not worried by his taking a stroll in the fresh air for five minutes when he knew I was embarking on a long question and answer session. Once, however, he was away for twenty minutes. He had suffered a bad attack of upset stomach, and had managed to block the headmistress's loo completely. He returned, somewhat green, to play for five minutes, only to vanish again for the rest of the performance. I finished alone.

In Sydney, where we gave the first double bass recital in the Opera House, our worst nightmare happened. Ansett Air lost half our luggage and, with it, half the music. We had a live broadcast the following morning and had to change the entire programme. As though this wasn't enough, we had to scour Sydney (on a Sunday) for clothes. When we returned to our flat after a very hectic day, we found a nocturnal pop group in the basement. We slept not a wink, and were forced to move out the next day.

Coda: On the way home, it took Mr Slatford 48 hours to get his double bass through customs at Bangkok.

It is in the South, where the sun exerts a gently addling influence, that Confusion trips out with a girlish giggle and scatters Chaos about like confetti. We start with:

Greece

and **Daniel Barenboim.**

It was on a tour with the English Chamber Orchestra in the early sixties. We played in Athens, and afterwards were booked to play in a little town in the north of Greece. It was a long trip – eight hours in a bus.

The orchestra had been to Lebanon after Athens, where I was not able to go. However, they brought me back a present – of an Arab head-dress. It was a very hot day, so I sat in the bus wearing bathing trunks and the head-dress. We arrived in the town in the late afternoon, and went to the square and had a drink. I was still in the same attire. Our manager went off to find the local concert producer. The promoter was impeccably dressed – black and white shoes, and a pearl in his tie. It took a long time to convince him that I was the conductor.

In due course, it was time to go to the amphitheatre, where the concert was happening. The piano was not there. It was on the way, the promoter assured us.

It arrived half an hour late. I took the lid off. The audience sat down. I gave an A for the orchestra. Or at least I did not, because each time I tried, my finger slid uncontrollably down the keyboard. I asked, "What is wrong?"

The promoter, hurt and earnest, said, 'Maestro, we cleaned the piano with the best Greek olive oil!'

(The compiler took this story down at great speed over the telephone from Bayreuth).

Emanuel Hurwitz was with the same team in the same country, but I do not think his story was of the same tour. He is concerned, too, about other aspects of the classical landscape:

We arrived in Athens from Beirut with delicate innards after a midnight reception in Baalbek. The Athens hotel was about at boiling point, and the room boasted an electric fan of the size that works off a small battery. I did not attend the afternoon rehearsal (the only one I have missed for health reasons!), and stretched out on my bed beside the miniscule fan...

The concert was well received and next morning at 8.30 we left for Volos, to play in a newly excavated amphitheatre. We arrived about 5 pm and started our rehearsal. The Greek summer day was still hot, and it was nice to run through the Bartok *Divertimento* while the platform was being built round us. When the piano for Daniel Barenhoim's Mozart Concerto was dragged on, it proved to be half a tone flat, and magnificently out of tune with itself. So, the concerto was abandoned, and a group of solos put in instead.

We had 45 minutes before the concert and were offered changing rooms in a nearby hotel. I enjoyed putting on my white tie and tails in a swimming pool cubicle, with wet bathers splashing around.

Then we were informed that we had to have a ceremonial dinner *before* the concert, as immediately after it our coach would drive us to our hotel, only two hours' journey. We had dinner and exchanged courteous toasts with Volos dignitaries in *eau minerale*. I think we got through the meal in 25 minutes flat.

Daniel's solos on the grilled piano were a pleasing artistic break for us. He included the Beethoven Turkish March, which no one noted as significant. At about 1 am we crept out of the coach to our hotel, which we would have to leave early next morning to get on to Salonika for the next concert. The hotel was still baking hot, even at this hour, and we were offered air conditioning (at a supplementary price), which was gratefully accepted.

The last thing I remember, as I lay down on the bed, was the jet of concrete dust being blown out of the air ducts.

Tunisia

TABARKA! The very word must be like a knell in management circles. It lies in Tunisia, somewhere near the Algerian border, and is, or was, one of the twin pillars of the Tabarka and Carthage Festival. Two of our contributors took artists there; **Basil Douglas** bringing **Ravi Shankar** and his percussion player in August 1973, and **Michael Vyner** the **London Sinfonietta** in August 1977. Nothing much seems to have changed in the inter-

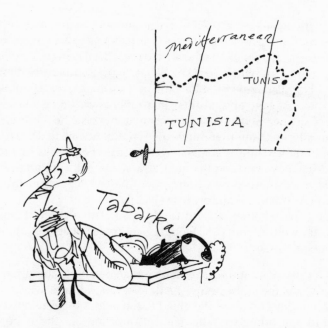

val except for the worse. Neither Mr Douglas nor Mr Vyner knows that the other has contributed to this book, which makes it all the more interesting for us to compare their accounts.

Both parties enjoyed the flight out. Both agree there. It was on landing at Tunis airport that their troubles began. In dealing with trouble from the natives, it might seem that Basil Douglas had a slight advantage. He had a light, mobile force, whereas Michael Vyner was leading a comparative army, some of it weighed down with heavy equipment in the bass clef. However, Basil Douglas had the handicap of a personal preoccupation: he had just been co-opted by Ravi Shankar into playing in the concert himself – on the tanpura, an Indian stringed instrument he had yet to learn, and which also meant he would have to be dressed for the occasion in Indian silk robes. It was a question of saving the concert – the instrument was essential for the ensemble, and the regular player was ill. Understandably, the prospect haunts his narrative like some ominous leitmotiv.

It was August, and Tunis airport as hot as an oven. The 'nice young man' who was to meet the London Sinfonietta and transfer them by bus to Tabarka (three hours away) was not there. Nor was the bus. The 'charming and intelligent' young man (were they the same person?) who was to meet Basil Douglas and party *was* there, but with a very small Fiat, supposed to carry himself, Basil Douglas, Ravi Shankar, the percussion player **Alla Rakha,** all their luggage and all their instruments including some very bulky drums. Sent away to find something else, he returned one hour later with another miniscule Fiat, but no one to drive it.

When the young man (if it was the same one), finally turned up for Michael Vyner and the orchestra, it was still without the bus. This took another two hours to come, while presumably the temperature in the airport rose steadily.

Both parties then set out for Tabarka. The orchestral journey was uneventful, but Basil Douglas, co-opted yet again, was at the wheel of the second Fiat:

> So I drive – a strange car in a strange, teeming, tumultuous city, on the right (wrong) side of the road, and without a driving licence; one eye glued to the rear of the Fiat in front, and the other swivelling in all directions in the hope of avoiding the beasts and the bicycles, the carts and the cars, all driven by cheerful maniacs, or so I think, but I don't have time to think. Not even of the tanpura. But somehow I manage, and away from the city the first glimpses of Africa are exciting...

One does not know how exciting they were for the London Sinfonietta; probably by then dusk had fallen on their enthusiasm.

Anyway, four Augusts apart, the two expeditions now converged on Tabarka itself. The London Sinfonietta were very late indeed. Michael Vyner takes up the story:

> ...we eventually found the Mimosas Hotel, which had, I was promised faithfully, reserved for us twenty single rooms with bath – and how all of us looked forward to that refreshing bath prior to a nice meal.
>
> As always, I went into the hotel, leaving the orchestra in the bus, to make sure all was well. To cut a long and very angry story short, the management of the hotel not only had

never heard of the London Sinfonietta or of those twenty single rooms with bath, but they had never heard of the Festival of Tabarka and Carthage. There I was, in the middle of a foreign and not terribly friendly country, with some of the most distinguished musicians of Britain, at night, after a day of travel, hungry and thirsty, and there was no hotel.

The orchestra spent the night on the beach, in huts belonging to a disused Club Méditerranée. Amenities were severe: communal lavatories, communal showers, no bedclothes, no pillows, no food and no drink. Going to sleep on a bare mattress, Michael Vyner dreamed of his mother telling him as a little boy to become a lawyer. His colleague and hut-mate, Anthony Whitworth-Jones slowly ate six grapes (the last of his ration), reading *The Times* under a naked light bulb.

They gave no concert in Tabarka. When Michael Vyner enquired the next day, no one in Tabarka knew about any concert that or any other evening, and the Carthage end of the Festival did not seem to care one way or the other what was happening in the sister town.

They did play their Carthage engagement, however, but only by dint of great resource. There was no official connection between Tabarka and Carthage by air, sea, or land. Anthony Whitworth-Jones leaped into a car apparently heading straight into the desert, to make the forward arrangements. Michael Vyner had to bribe a private individual to take the rest of them there in a bus.

This, their one Festival concert, was in the open air theatre in Carthage – the audience consisting of the Corps Diplomatique and government ministers. The British Ambassador looked at Michael Vyner with deep understanding, as he recounted his misadventures. Michael Vyner concludes:

On Friday, 12th August, we departed Tunis Airport, arriving at Heathrow in the afternoon, with a feeling of gladness and happiness which I had never experienced before. I invited Anthony to my home for a meal and, during the first course, I remember bursting into tears. Everything seemed so delicious, so friendly, so secure; I suppose it must have been sheer relief.

You might like to know that the Tunisian authorities paid us in full for the two concerts, even though only one was performed, and you might also like to know that in the entire history of the London Sinfonietta, that was the only concert that was not played.

Back in Tabarka, the Hotel Morjatte was not expecting Basil Douglas and his party either. A cold Festival official eventually materialised, and rooms were at length prepared. If there was no hotel for the London Sinfonietta, it is doubtful whether they missed much. The beach-hut amenities might have been primitive, but some were unspeakable here. Also the air-conditioning did not work. What food there was, was hard to come by, and for what drink there was, there were no glasses.

The Festival office started by trying to reduce the artists' fees, because the regular tanpura player had not come. This cannot have encouraged Basil Douglas, practising away assiduously on the instrument. Then a gale blew up, meaning that the concert, already sold out, would have to be given in the night-club of the hotel, seating 300, instead of the open air stadium, seating 2000.

In the event, the concert was a wild success. The police had to clear a gangway in the sardine-packed night-club for the artists to get on the stage. Basil Douglas, billed by Ravi Shankar as 'London's greatest tanpura player' acquitted himself well. His only difficulty was in getting up off the floor at the end of the concert.

The return home, idyllic for Michael Vyner, was not so for this party. First, the young man (he was called Khalled) again arrived with two cars and no driver for the second. This time Basil Douglas refused the job, and a 'cousin' was found to fill the breach. Artists and manager spent a luxurious night at the Majestic Hotel in Tunis, with all the party conviviality of those going home the next day.

Unfortunately, next morning Khalled failed to turn up to drive the artists to the airport. As he was also supposed to pay the hotel bill, the hotel refused to release the luggage. A deal was made, by which Basil Douglas, luckily on a later flight, was allowed to see his artists off at the airport, provided he left his own suitcase behind as hostage. With some difficulty, the party elbowed its way through to Departures – then, just at the moment the two musicians were passing through the barrier, Khalled appeared, having overslept and been arrested for speeding, with a car licence twelve years out of date.

An interlude followed. The hotel bill was paid. Basil Douglas went for a stroll in the Old City. Khalled vanished at high speed for Tabarka, and Basil Douglas stepped into a Festival car to catch his own plane. The car broke down immediately. Now without any Tunisian money, he threatened to expose the driver to his employers unless he found him a taxi, and paid for it himself. To his surprise, this worked, and he just made the flight for Paris. The story does not end there... The plane from Paris to London caught fire!

There has to be one good sequel to all this, and there is. **Vlado Perlemuter,** white with nerves just before going on to play the Beethoven C minor Piano Concerto at the Royal Albert Hall (the end of Basil Douglas's journey) was so overcome with laughter at his agent's story, that he forgot his fears, and gave a stunning performance.

Envoi: *In the Steps of Columbus*

Katharine Hart, viola, was with the London Chamber Orchestra, on a tour which, like the movie *Jaws*, started as an idyll and then turned into something else.

The orchestra was making a pioneering tour of the Caribbean and district. Beautiful days on the beach in Jamaica and Trinidad, then the next leg – Bogota by way of Caracas. The plane headed towards the Venezuelan mountains, and began going down for the landing, when an appalling storm broke, thunder and lightning, everything. The plane suddenly dropped a thousand feet, then equally suddenly veered up at right angles into the sky. The mountains loomed close – nobody knew what was happening or where they were going. The London Chamber Orchestra were very frightened indeed. Around them, emotional Latins were screaming and crossing themselves.

The pilot made a macho attempt to land at Caracas airport, which was closed. Luckily he was persuaded there was no need for him to die with all his passengers for the honour of the airline. It would be quite all right if he landed at Curaçao instead. This he did, thank goodness, and the orchestra spent a shaken night at the home of orange liqueur. Next day they made Caracas, and flew on to Bogota. To everyone's relief, there was no repetition of the previous day's horror in the air.

Thankful to be on terra firma, they had a good dinner, and went to bed. They had just lain down, when Bogota was struck by an earthquake. Miss Hart's bed rolled about like a yacht in high seas, the pictures went askew on the walls, lights crashed down. The chamber-maid had hysterics, and in the corridors, emotional Southerners were again screaming and crossing themselves.

When the hotel stopped waving about, there was orchestral unison on one thing. This was the worst forty-eight hours they had spent in their lives. Indeed, I believe it has gone down in musical annals as almost the nastiest little tour of all time.

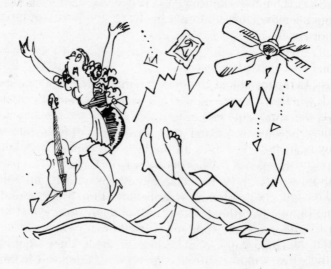

Turkish Delights

Because of pre-concert nerves, artists like to know whereabouts in the 'venue' the loo can be located. **Moura Lympany** asked where it was when she was performing at a concert in one of the Anglo-Turkish Music Festivals (now, alas, discontinued) at Ankara. She was directed down a corridor. She opened one door, to find a small room which consisted of a hole in the floor, and no visible means of support. She concluded that must be the Gents, and tried the next, which had to be the Ladies, to find another hole in the floor. Both were the same, and it was explained to her that such was the situation *alla turca*. Her difficulty was that she was wearing a Dior blue tulle frock with a *train*. This made the situation even more complicated than it was already. Asia Minor adopts a somewhat lordly attitude to women, and it is not going to alter the design of such services to accommodate women as distinct from men, let alone anything as outlandish as a girl with a train.

Miss Lympany asked the Festival organiser, one Tom Eastwood, whether he would come in, and hold the train. He replied "Love, the Turks wouldn't understand." What a totally ungallant reaction! Ask me that again now, and there would be no such callow hesitation. To hell if the Turks understood or not. Some compromise was reached, Tom Eastwood in the corridor, probably holding on to some piece of Miss Lympany's train, his other hand ready to intercept any misunderstanding Turk.

Miss Lympany went on stage to give her recital, which started with the Bach Chromatic Fantasy and Fugue. The piano was right at the back of the platform, which meant she was playing into the wings and the curtains. She went off to find someone to help her push it forward, but there was no one. She returned to the piano and tried to push it herself. This time, a little more gallantry was in evidence. Six men jumped on to the stage from the audience, and hauled the piano into position.

All proceeded well, until the slow movement of the Chopin B

minor Sonata. Miss Lympany had recently become engaged, and her husband-to-be had given her two diamond clips as a present, before she went on this tour. They were fastened to the top of her dress, but not fast enough. At the most pianissimo passage, in this still and intense movement, one of them fell off, and jumped musically along the platform. Inevitably, titters started in the audience. (Kemal Ataturk would have curled his lip in amusement). Faced with another Gallipoli, especially should the other clip fall off as well, Miss Lympany froze all movement save that of her hands. She went on playing, and the stillness of the moment, together with her refusal to give way, quietened the audience. Bravery in action is something they respect out there. "Dişi aslan gibi!" they would have said to themselves as they applauded. "Like a lioness!"

From what I remember these festivals were not without various misunderstandings and mauvais moments. The publicity for one of them went a little haywire when a photograph of Benjamin Britten appeared in a newspaper over the caption 'Mr Peter Grimes'. On another occasion, a visiting conductor, confronted by a Turkish score with a sequence of time signature changes like 5/4 3/16 2/2 9/8 7/4, threw his baton across the room exclaiming "They're trying to make a fool of me!"

Two Proms

It is a rare honour for an artist to be engaged as a soloist in two promenade concerts in the same week. Proms are important dates, and **Iona Brown** was aware of the seriousness and responsibility of these two occasions.

The first Prom was on a Tuesday, and she was to play the Walton Violin Concerto with the BBC Symphony Orchestra. It was a live broadcast, and the house was packed. Miss Brown sailed through the first two movements, but somewhere in the first thirty bars of the last movement, *the* horror happened – a string snapped. It was the E string: Miss Brown's reaction was one of sharp and sudden shock, followed by an overwhelming desire to run away. Panic overcome, with great presence of mind, she passed her violin to the leader, **Rodney Friend,** and took his in exchange. Meanwhile, one of the violinists would replace her string. This would have been a good idea but for the fact that Mr Friend's violin had a huge shoulder rest, which put everything out of true for her: she had to master, almost on the instant, a completely different technique of playing. And no one seemed to want to change her string. She glanced longingly back at her instrument during the various tuttis and saw it being passed further and further back through the first violins, like a hot potato. The final part of the concerto, intense and technically dazzling (the work was written for Heifetz), was looming near, and the prospect of tackling that on a violin she had never played before was terrifying.

Just in the nick of time her own instrument was passed forward and forward and forward, and was returned to her. Unfortunately, the little ring that protects the E string from the bridge was not on the bridge where it should be, but buzzing up and down on the string itself, making it impossible to play. With the lightning speed of self-preservation, she pushed it down to the extreme other end of the instrument, and managed to finish. There was wild applause.

Two days later was her second concert. She got up, dreading the reviews of the first, but they were good. Even so she thought: "What if it happens again? Pray God it doesn't happen again." People will not be impressed, she thought. Breaking a string once is all right, but in two successive Proms it could be taken by the humourless as disrespect.

She played Vaughan Williams's *The Lark Ascending*, for the second Prom. It was going very well, as larks go. "God is on my side," she thought, "the E string is going to hold." It did, and just as well with those long, unaccompanied high altitude phrases. Then came the decisive moment. The orchestra stopped, and she took off on her final flight into the stratosphere.

There seemed no reason for anyone to scream, but they did. They went on screaming. They screamed and screamed, regular punchy screams, from one of the boxes. "Shall I ignore it?" she asked herself. She decided to play louder. A purist might argue that if Vaughan Williams had wanted a loud lark, he would have written one. On the other hand, if you have a woman screaming against a very high note on the E string, it is better to mark it up a bit.

Miss Brown played the final outer-space notes as loud as she could. It was a high risk enterprise, as one can get the 'purlies' (the compiler does not know what they are, but he quotes Miss Brown), and she held the vibrato as long as she dared. The woman went on screaming. She was having a baby in the box.

Wrong Concerto

To arrive at the concert hall having prepared the wrong work must be a favourite nightmare among soloists. Perhaps they mercifully wake up, and are spared the awful sequel, which is that they must then play the right one, and they may not even know it. The hands go damp, even at the thought. The only consolation is that it happens to the best of us – and in reality, not in the safety of dreams. The message of these two stories is of a wondrous professionalism.

Vladimir Ashkenazy

Many years ago I played in Israel with the Israel Philharmonic Orchestra and Zubin Mehta. It is usual on such visits to Israel for an artist to play twelve to thirteen concerts practically every day save Fridays. Usually one plays two or three different concertos.

That time I played Beethoven 2 and Beethoven 3. I think I played six times the one, and six times the other. They alternated rather chaotically – I would be playing three nights in a row No. 2, then the next day No. 3, and the following day No. 2 again, then twice No 3, etc. Zubin Mehta knew No. 3 by memory, but No. 2 he conducted for the first time and he needed the score, even for the performances subsequent to the first night.

The funny thing happened on the eighth or ninth night. We came to the concert thinking it was No. 2 that night (as was typed in our itineraries). Just before going on the platform we joked to each other – is it No. 2 or No. 3? – and both agreed it was indeed No. 2. We were overheard by the personnel manager of the orchestra, who was standing at the door, and waiting to open it for us to go to the stage. He said: "No, it is No. 3 tonight." We laughed, being sure he was kidding us. After all, our itineraries said No. 2. But he said "I am serious, it *is* No. 3." Anyway, we shrugged our shoulders and went on stage.

The first thing we discovered was that there was no conductor's stand, meaning no score. Zubin, still sure it must be No. 2, decided that people in charge thought that by now he knew No. 2 well enough not to need the score – and did not bother to put the stand on. So he crossed himself, and gave a strong upbeat for the opening bar of No. 2. The orchestra played ... No. 3. Zubin was so taken aback when he heard No. 3 that he stopped conducting for a while, but the orchestra continued playing.

It was a good performance after that, but we laughed a lot afterwards. Our itineraries were wrong!

Ida Haendel

I was in the midst of an Australian tour in 1982, when my London manager called me long distance, asking whether I could step in for Isaac Stern, who was suddenly indisposed. Programme: Bartok's Violin concerto.

Although basically I don't like to replace any artist, the circumstances were unusual. Isaac Stern happens to be a friend as is Daniel Barenboim, who was to conduct the concert of the Orchestre de Paris. I accepted, asking however to play Brahms instead, as I hadn't played Bartok in a decade at least. My manager explained that this was impossible – it was a Bartok festival. I took Concorde from New York, and arrived in Paris late at night to find the contract waiting for me at the hotel – programme: Brahms and Bartok.

In the morning, I met with Barenboim at the rehearsal, who took one look at the Bartok score which I had brought, and exclaimed, horrified, "It's the wrong Bartok! It should be No. 1!" Since I had never played Bartok No. 1, nor even heard it performed by anybody, this was a problem indeed. At the sight of Mr Barenboim's hysteria however, I calmly ordered them to bring me the score of No. 1.

I played the unknown (to me) concerto, to a packed Salle Pleyel, plus the Brahms, hypnotising myself into the belief that I had played the Bartok a dozen times.

Nobody knew the difference.

Wrong Conductor

Sir Yehudi Menuhin

In a German city, which shall be nameless, I gave a performance of the Beethoven Violin Concerto with an orchestra, which shall also be nameless, and a conductor, also nameless, who was absolutely dreadful.

In desperation I finally asked him if he would perhaps follow what he heard. This proved somewhat difficult for him. I vowed, therefore, that when the tutti came at the end I should take my own tempo. I did, and the first desks came with me. We finished eight bars ahead of the conductor and the rest of the orchestra, whereupon half the audience applauded. The other half waited until our colleagues came to the end.

I braced myself, but, to my astonishment, no one booed – but then the Germans have always been a self-disciplined nation!

Wrong Connections

Probably the most complicated concert on record was given by **Gillian Weir** on the organ of the magnificent new concert hall in Melbourne.

Such is our passion for reproducing the past with all its inconveniences, that the organ was built as a faithful copy of an old instrument. Wilfully anachronistic, it has no aids to play, so Miss Weir needed two assistants to be able to give a proper performance. It is also oddly positioned. If there is a concerto to play (and there was) the organist cannot see the conductor. So closed-circuit television has to be installed. This helps the organist, but not the conductor, because he, poor man, cannot see the organ at all. It is completely hidden, and at such a height that there is an enormous time lag before what it plays actually reaches the ear. All in all, it is not surprising there was a disastrous first rehearsal. Television alone was not deemed adequate as a reliable link. It was decided to give Miss Weir headphones as well, working from a microphone placed near the first violin. To make sure, a buzzer system was added, so that Miss Weir, now wired up like an old fashioned robot, could let the stage manager know she was ready to begin. The stage manager would then signal the conductor to give the down beat... All the advantages of modern technology were there, to hinder Miss Weir.

She bowed to the audience from her eyrie, then went to the bench, got her dress arranged, got her two assistants arranged, put on her headphones, and was just pulling out the stops on the organ, when to her horror she heard the orchestra begin. The buzzer had gone off by itself, and the conductor had started. She missed her entry, and the ghastliness of this was mirrored in the anguished face of the conductor on her closed-circuit television screen. For all he knew, since it was not two-way, she might have left the building, or been electrocuted, and, having missed one entry, he had no idea if or when she was going to make another. She came in on the next, but the performance was ruined. They were both furious with each other. As they took their bows (which involved Miss Weir running down two flights of stairs, with people holding doors open), they smiled at one another, uttering mutual recriminations through clenched teeth. Embracing and holding hands on stage, they agreed it was the most ridiculous situation they had ever been in, and stalked off to their separate dressing-rooms.

Out of this came the decision that, for the next performance, there would also have to be a talk-back system, so that the conductor would not begin even if the buzzer went off. Miss Weir now had a television screen, headphones, a buzzer, two assistants and a talk-back. It was absolutely ridiculous. There had been no chance to check the talk-back system, nor the level or the balance of the headphones. While the orchestra played away at Beethoven No.5, people were crawling around Miss Weir in the organ loft whispering "OK" and making adjustments. They got the level right. The Beethoven, which was the piece before her concerto, finished. Then the headphones faded out completely.

Masked by the applause for the Beethoven, a tense drama started. Miss Weir screamed in a whisper to the stage manager through the talk-back "Margaret! Margaret!" trying to tell her the headphones had gone. Margaret did not hear, but in the end telephoned. Miss Weir said the headphones had died. Margaret said "What headphones?" There followed an unprintable interlude. The headphones were restored. "Sorry," the stage manager whispered over the telephone, though there was no need to whisper at that end, "Somebody kicked the switch."

And so they got through another performance . . .